WRECKING BALL PRESS
HULL • ISSUE 3

the reater

EDITOR & WHIP CRACKER

SHANE RHODES

Design & Cover Illustration   by   Owen Benwell

With special thanks to: Jules Smith •   Ian Parks •
• The very reverend Newdick • Russell Jones

This edition of the reater has been part funded by the editor.
Wrecking Ball Press gratefully acknowledges the financial help of
Yorkshire Arts & Kingston Upon Hull City Council

All submissions, subscriptions,
and any other material should be sent to :
The Reater
18 Church Street
North Cave
Brough
East Yorkshire
HU15 2LW

Published in 1999 by Wrecking Ball Press

table of contents

brendan cleary
the lodger..13
peter...14
after the party...15
the stranger..16
fireworks...17
the photograph..18
blue...19

gerald locklin
william hogarth: a rake's progress:
the tavern scene...23
david hockney:
the road to york through sledmere............................24
dirty old men and the new double standard..................26
are the social police misrepresenting
their constituency?..27
the corner grocery...28

khan singh kumar
she turns down her ticket to the homeland...................41
catcall...42
when the social worker came back for more.................43

peter knaggs
phlegm..47
seat still warm...48
the radio..49
just to let you know..50

(picture by david hernandez)

k. m. dersley
them and their postures..55

roddy lumsden
my realm of the senses...63
my dark side...64
drummond...65

scarlet..66
communion..67

joan jobe smith
wired!!...71
married to the machinist..72
mack the maniac..73
poem from the los angeles county gaol...................75

labi siffre
economedy 2..79
mantra...80
benediction...81

lisa glatt
my sweetest piece..85
the atheist's tunnel..86
spaz...88

carol coiffait
monsieur magritte berates the beatles......................93
short cut..95
dog story...96

(picture by david hernandez)

tricia cherin
grand central station..101
meaning making...102

charles bukowski
charles bukowski's first ever published interview.........107

sean burn
16:x...117
trans pennine..120

devreaux baker
nights and the north sea..125
homesick..126
myself greets you...127
learning how to dance..128

jules smith
the man who shot simon armitage.............................133

(picture by david hernandez)

rodney wood
history...143
looking straight ahead - robert mitchum.............144

fred voss
they know how to protect their own.................149
high wires and ticking clocks.........................150
birth at the mouth of the blast furnace.............151
all the perfectly tied shoelaces....................152
and we didn't have to die to get there.............153
dissertation on a drop of sweat.....................154
trying to keep our feet on planet earth.............156
drop hammers and dilated eyes.......................157
gods that tick and blast and beep...................158
fan shortage..159

richard whelan
community service blues.............................163
pain threshold......................................164
stock answer..165

greta stoddart
switzerland...169
pegasus...171
the no. 4...172
to day..173

maurice rutherford
his letter she'd kept...............................177
waterloo bridge.....................................178

(picture by david hernandez)

james prue
no. 17 retford place................................183
not quite grown up no. 1............................184
bastards..185

ben myers
the greek girl's arse...189
bobby and the seven dogs' tails..........................191
literary rejections are what make a man.............192
the contract..193

simon armitage
the flags of the nations....................................195

david hernandez
death wish...196

charles bennet
william wordsworth's socks...............................197

b. a. j. evans
almost...198

a. a. dodd
white christmas and cold turkey........................200

dave wright
eldorado..201

gordon mason
a laying - on of hands......................................202

ian parks
promises and smiles...203

andrew parker
straightener...204

michael curran
who needs rain in the afternoon.........................205

dean wilson
get your cock out my arse
i can feel a poem coming on..............................206

daithidh maceochaidh
traidhg ruadh takes off his trilby.......................208

jon summers
alive, alright..209

janet oliver
down the pit..210

fiona curran
the incomplete inventory................................211

denise duhamel
no home - wrecker..215
snapshots from a stolen camera....................216

david lyall
cut and dried..221
the lovers..222
waiting..223

(picture by david hernandez)

raymond robinson
migratory birds...229
and your tongue fills your mouth..................230

mark mckain
next time...239
satin...240

geoff hattersley
handshake poem..245
alex..246
before and after midnight.............................247
y'know warramean......................................248
ride..249
randy newman et al.....................................250
like harpo marx..251
the valdez blues..252
at this table in huddersfield.........................253

reviews.........255

(picture by david hernandez)

brendan cleary

Newcastle, England

The Lodger

& if my name were Robert De Niro
it wouldn't change anything, a jot,
tonight I'm the gooseberry again.

She wants him bad & I don't care,
I just want my bed, ham sandwiches,
& we have to share but I get none.

The new lodger, cosmic go-between,
fetcher & carrier, the socialite,
they'd be knackered without me.

This isn't the new deal I signed for,
it's not what I imagined, a boy scout.
Oh fortune's course you disturb me!

& anytime they will be at the shagging,
he shags her, she shags him, I shudder,
if the girls in the office saw me now....

Peter

Peter got carted off but he did speak sense once,
I can't remember exactly when but he definitely did.

He fed the swans on the lake amphetamine sulphate,
they danced about, fluttered, keeled over & died.

What a big surprise this was to Peter & his wife,
she's called 'Sorry I took this route in my life'

which doesn't particularly roll off the tongue, does it?.....

After The Party

My newspaper shook, words turning Catalan,
the day the Giant Bee followed me around.

I tried to shake off its shadow looming
over my shoulder in mischief as I quaked,

mumbling some guide book phrases
picked up on that trip to Barcelona.

'Por Favor', 'Aqua con gas' didn't work
as I staggered through North Laines.

I tried Aspirin, I tried Cola & Ice Cream,
I tried reciting the Rosary but to no avail.

The Giant Bee had circled in to swallow me,
I knew it for sure but how could I mention it?....

The Stranger

The stranger & I talked
of rare moths & gravity.

He showed me the tattoo
of an ostrich on his leg.

I told him about sleeping
in a phone box once, upright.

So the beers flowed & ebbed
& can you imagine my surprise

when the stranger vomited
profusely all over my shoes

when I asked him back to mine
to scrape off some wallpaper,

maybe torture next door's cat?.....

Fireworks

On the night of the fireworks
we ran out of the pub to see

a kaleidoscope of flares & red
blossoms erupting from the pier.

Later you forgot your name again
so I fetched the officers to help.

Thankfully they knew your identity
when they found heroin in your hair.....

The Photograph

In the second-hand heaven
of the North Laines in June

I bought a photo of a priest.
He was smiling next to a tree,

doubtless he was sharing a joke
with the young curate I imagine

uncertain of his vocation yet,
his head full of choir-girls

& the Holy Ghost talking to him
when he sleeps or when he wakes.

It was kinda sinister that photo,
& used to transport me too often.

Once the priest hadn't really laughed
but was faking & the curate had died.

Once the choir-girls all appeared
they danced about on only one leg.

Round about then the sun turned sour
& insects came in droves into my dreams.....

Blue

Sometimes richer than the sky
or maybe its shade in my head

when my transistor has broken
& the bank own my lopsided bed.

Blue could be when I think of her
or when I realise I never do anymore.

Bluesmen serenade me on the circuit
of my brain, what I eat can make it.

Or I can be blue when I'm happy too,
when I know your smooth cheek I stroke

will wither & I'm Bluer than Blue can be
at the thought of us not around to picnic.....

gerald locklin
Long Beach, USA

William Hogarth: a rake's progress: the tavern scene

the men were never outnumbered
10 to 2 by the women
in the taverns i hung out in.
nearly bare bosoms weren't in vogue either,
although i guess some bars held weekly
wet tee-shirt contests.
i guess you could have caught the clap
if you tried hard enough,
but none of us had enough money
in our pockets for anyone
to bother picking them.
purses for men hadn't come back into
style yet. the beer was cheap;
the wine a joke. so was the pool table,
and there were women before the women's movement
who could shoot a better stick
than most of the men.
a certain amount of petty gambling went on--
cards, dice, sports--but periodically the
agents of the alcoholic beverage control
would crack down on it. no, the taverns
weren't a good place to get laid in my day--
the maleness of them scared most women off--
and it was just looking for trouble
to bring your own woman in.
a few women enjoyed them, though, like having
entree to a world where more fun was being had.

now these places are largely gone or changed.
three things killed them: feminism, cocaine,
and the new puritanism. and a lot of the drinkers
of my generation ended up dead, broke, or,
like me, on the wagon. so there's
no big temptation to return to that world,
because it's no longer there.

we lasted longer, though,
than the dumbshit rake did.

23

David Hockney:
the road to york through sledmere

i've walked the roads
into the heart of villages.
be sure to look both ways,
right and left, right and wrong,

before you cross the road. the
lorries have been lifted from
this scene. you are the lorry.
you're the man from mars,

the ancient astronaut, come
back to see how things have
fared. you trusted that your
deeds would last a while here

and they did. the oldest thing
is usually the churchyard, and
the living grow back centuries
as well. every village has its

war memorial. every village has
its color. this one's red as
oklahoma clay. high walls make
best neighbors. chimneys keep

us cozy. god is green. don't
speed on through to york. you'll
only find more walls there. virtual
medieval. markets where the markets

were. a lump of danish horseshit pet-
rified. pub lunch at club med(ieval).
medicinal (real) ale. stay a moment
for a parlor tea in sledmere. have

your pub lunch here, a shepherd's.
breathe blue smoke, the strong crust
of friendly breath. listen to syllables
wrestled up from roughened throats,

tasted, chewed, and gently spat
like turf. mud is an absolute.
stand still an afternoon here.
you'll probably be in a rush

to get home, next time through.

dirty old men and the new double standard

bukowski was right to
apply the term to himself
before anyone else could.
he always had a knack for
launching pre-emptive strikes,
although they were sometimes unnecessary,
even downright paranoid.
but i'm sure he would have been accused
by the envious
of being a dirty old man
if he hadn't already blithely applied
the label to himself.

the problem is i've never understood
what is supposed to be dirty:
is being old dirty?
is being old and sexual dirty?
is being old and sexual and finding
the young attractive dirty?
would it be okay for us to call
a mature woman
who was sexual with a much younger man
a dirty old woman?
an old slut?

or would we be expected to treat her
as some sort of heroic model
of female self-realization?

maybe the dirty old women
don't want to compete with younger women
for the attentions of
the dirty old men.

are the social police misrepresenting their constituency?

in spite of the current reign of terror,
i still compliment women on their appearances:

a colorful new outfit,
a fresh hairdo,
a tan,
a little weight loss (although this
one can be risky).

it seems the natural thing to do,
the friendly thing,
and i don't follow up
with an invitation to lunch.

i sometimes wonder if
it will get me in hot water, but,
so far, no woman has seemed anything other than
quite visibly pleased to be complimented
on her comely appearance.

The Corner Grocery

They call them "Junior Markets" out here. They are convenience stores whose sales are mainly beer and wine. Some of them have full liquor licenses, but the one on the highway just outside our tract never has. Maybe that's one reason it has a history of going out of business. Maybe it's because the mini-mall it's in is just too "mini"--the parking lot is so small that there's an exaggerated risk of fender-benders. Maybe some of its business overlaps with the donut shop next door. Maybe some of the previous owners didn't *want* to make money--maybe it was some kind of a front or they were involved in money laundering or something. *I* know a massive underground economy exists in my country, but its intricacies are as much beyond my comprehension as are those of the so-called legitimate economy. I have never really been a part of either. English teachers are not supposed to be a part of an economy--we are not supposed to understand economies. Those of us who understand money are regarded with suspicion, especially by the creative writing students. Fortunately, I have never displayed any signs of financial savvy. Obviously no one with any fiscal smarts would be caught dead shopping in such overpriced venues as neighborhood grocery stores.

I missed the corner grocery the last time that it was shut down, a period of over a year. I hadn't patronized it much because I was still drinking in those days and, as I said, it didn't stock hard booze or foreign beers or decent wines. It was pretty much of an emporium for Bud and Boone's Farm. And I'd purchased canned goods that had proved to be years past their sell-by dates. Canned chili does not improve with age. But it was good to have a place nearby if you ran out of toilet paper, Tylenol, or charcoal. And, the eternal optimist, I kept expecting it to improve, would drop hints of items I would love to see in stock, marketing suggestions that raised not the heavy lids of the listless, unenfranchised clerks. So I was mildly heartened to observe, driving by on the way home from a department meeting, a banner announcing its imminent re-opening under the proverbial new management.

It opened with almost as bare shelves as it had closed with, but the new man behind the counter, middle-aged, with an unostentatious moustache and a foreign accent, was much more eager to accommodate. "Diet iced tea," I would ask, because I had now quit drinking and was under doctor's orders to lose weight," and he would take out a small pad and say, "I will get you some." "Kellogg's Raisin Bran?" A week later there were stacks of it. "Non-fat milk?" "Tell me what you'd like and I will stock it for you."
"But what if no one else buys it?"
"You are a regular customer," he said; "you are one of my first customers. I want to stock things for my loyal customers." That almost drove me away. I have never handled obligations well, as evidenced by my marital history, and I really couldn't afford to do all my shopping there, but I wanted to see the place do well, and the healthier items *did* appear on the shelves, and so I bit the bullet and pulled into the lethal parking lot more often than I really should have.

I always forgot to pick up a basket when I entered. I would end up at the cash register with boxes and bottles protruding perilously from my grasp. At first he would remind me of the baskets, bright red and donated, judging from the stickers, by the generous Marlboro people. Then he began bringing one to me. "Are you walking?" he would ask; "Take one home with you. If you ever want to pay with a check, feel free to do so. If you want to make the check for more than the amount, that's fine."

He even began to give me discounts: "I will only charge you a dollar for that," he would say. "Thank you, but you don't have to do that," I'd reply, but frankly I was grateful. I even took to timing my arrivals for when he was behind the counter. The quiet woman, younger than himself, also foreign, who sometimes worked in his stead, was perfectly polite but she did not know about the discounts. So if I happened in on her shift, I purchased only what was absolutely necessary.
I hope I have not given the impression this man was a fool. I never considered him so. He gave every indication of knowing his business, of understanding the value of creating good will,

and of a core clientele. I had known bar owners who had underestimated these principles and others who had, to their detriment, forgotten them. After all, I did spend more there than I had ever intended to. And he knew by now, from my checks, that I lived in the neighborhood and taught at the local university. And, as with a restaurant, it is not good for a store to appear always empty. Success breeds success. And empty places are more apt to be held up. He was no fool.

On the other hand, he was not purely calculating either. He was of an ancient people who were capable of kindness. I figured he was either Middle Eastern or of the subcontinent. I thought the latter. When I asked him if he'd ever lived in England, he for the first time showed just the slightest hardness in his eyes, as if I were intruding where it was none of my business. Or perhaps he was remembering bad times there--I had forgotten tales of Paki-bashing. At any rate I hastened to assure him that I had simply been in England for stretches of time myself there, knew that there was a large Pakistani population there, and had in fact learned to eat Indian and Pakistani food there, which my wife and I now often drive the ten miles to Artesia for, the Southern California square-mile Little India. I recounted the first time I ate curry in Earl's Court, ordering the spiciest variety because I thought I'd been prepared for it by salsa, and almost sweated and hiccuped myself to death. We discussed regional differences of cuisine. He seemed reassured.

The next time I stopped by he told me he was going to prepare food for myself and my family. I didn't know whether he meant to invite us to dinner or to bring food to the store for us to heat at home. I was caught off guard and did not encourage him. I seldom socialize and my wife and I socialize with others together on only the rarest of occasions. I foresaw disasters. I shifted the conversation to the availability of frozen varieties of Indian food, and whether he intended to stock chutney. I'm sure I hurt his feelings--my implicit rejection of his hospitality may have been a serious rebuff in his culture, a painful loss of face. But to have done otherwise would have been merely postponing an eventual catastrophe. He did not speak of it again. I still feel bad about

30

it, and I know I drew a line that day which neither of us would ever cross, but it was unavoidable. No doubt he had survived worse in his life. Probably he attributed it to race. It was not--I simply did not desire to cultivate family friendships with anyone. My private life is full and complicated and I need time for my work. Best friends have never been inside my house. It doesn't matter how he interpreted it. I could not be any other way. I am not at this point in my life interested in broadening my horizons or extending my social life. We would still be friends within the confines of the store. I was still a loyal customer.

We have skinheads in the neighborhood, kids from the nearby high school, or dropouts therefrom, or recent graduates. They gather together in what they no doubt think of as a gang, get drunk and hurl beer bottles at their backyard walls and threaten "to kill themselves a nigger." They are much more likely to be killed than to kill. No doubt they deal drugs to each other. Some of them end up in rehab programs. They are not intellectual luminaries. They do not add to the comfort of the neighborhood, especially since there is an interracial couple, graduate students, who keep a low profile, living across the street. Still, while I abhor racism, I understand the frustrations of these white kids and their feeling that they need to band together. The blacks and the chicanos, the Vietnamese, Cambodians, and Chinese all have their gangs--why shouldn't the whites? Nor are whites the only racists anymore. Their sense of being themselves victims of discrimination may not be entirely a matter of perception. The skinhead phenomenon is deplorable, and a source of tension in the neighborhood, but it was certainly predictable.

I saw a couple of carloads of them pull up in front of the corner grocery store one day. Some went inside and some stayed in the cars. From my own car I jotted down their license plates. I have a terrible visual memory but I did my best to notice a few of their physical details beyond the shaved heads. When they seemed to have been in the store too long, I got out of the car and went inside myself. But I found no sign that they'd planned a robbery or any violence. They seemed just to be shopping for after-school snacks. Maybe they were doing some petty shoplifting. It would be hard to keep an eye on all of them. A lot of that must go on in any corner grocery. My friend had a bemused expression on his face, but did not seem overly concerned.

For a while he had a couple of young people working there. But then one morning I saw in the newspaper that a string of places had been cited by the Alcoholic Beverage Control for selling to minors. The corner grocery was one of them. The young clerks ceased to be employed there. When I asked my friend about it, he said that they'd been unable to say no to their buddies. The offense would not be repeated. Signs went up warning juveniles. A sign also appeared of a store-keeper brandishing an outsized shotgun. The face of my friend was superimposed.

I realized I did not know his name. But I didn't ask. It would have seemed an intrusion.

He called me "Professor." I hate to be called "Professor" or "Prof" or "Doc" but I didn't correct him. He seemed to be comfortable with it.

He acquired a Lotto machine. I had always purchased my Lotto tickets next door in the donut shop, but now I bought them in the grocery. The donut shop didn't need my business. I told myself that maybe it would change my luck. It didn't.

Then the new Lotto machine broke. It took the state three months to fix it. The corner store had a low priority on repairs because it didn't do enough volume.
"How are you supposed to sell more tickets with a broken machine?" He smiled and shrugged. That seemed to be his response to setbacks in general. I could have used a little of that calm myself. I wondered what his religion was, if he was still religious. But I didn't ask. Whatever it was or wasn't, it probably boiled down to the religion of experience and maybe of genetic predisposition. I don't understand why we are the way we are any better than I understand economics, but I figure we

are probably the way we have to be, the way life makes us. Those of us who survive at least. Like everyone else, I have my theories. I try them out, discard some, retain others, modify them as I go. And like all of us I will die knowing nothing, certainly not whether I was born for a reason, or whether anything awaits me, or why I was the way I was.

I think, though, that I buy my Lotto tickets (now that the machine is finally fixed) at the corner grocery rather than at the donut shop because I like the proprietor more. The owners of the donut shop are Asian. I don't know if they are Japanese or Vietnamese or Chinese or Cambodian. I don't know if it matters. She is younger than he is. Neither of them ever smiles. The two of them are always in the shop. I'm sure they work incredibly long hours. I have read articles on how the members of the recent Asian immigrant communities help each other to make it in the donut business. They have become serious competitors to Winchell's. I admire this. I am from a background of Irish immigrants and they made it the same way, sticking together, helping each other out, working long, hard hours, saving their money, limiting their own horizons while expanding those of my generation. It is the story of America.

But the people in the donut shop never smile at me. They don't know how to joke with me. They try to get me to buy more Lotto tickets than I want. They try to get me to buy donuts when I don't want donuts. And their raisin-bran muffins, which are what I buy if I am buying only for myself, are, finally, not very good.

And so I prefer to buy my Lotto tickets from the man in the grocery store, although I do not think one can extrapolate from this to a preference for the peoples of the subcontinent over those of the Far East. The people in the donut shop may, for instance, have been boat people. God knows what they may have endured.

The Irish were, of course, boat people also. But not my generation. I do not, however, forget that I am not far removed from immigrant routes, even as I wonder, in the manner of the settled, the nativist, whether California can survive its current waves of immigration.

In England the Indians and Pakistanis seem preferred to the West Indians and Irish. They are considered more industrious. Perhaps they just absorbed more English culture in colonial times. Perhaps they were better treated by the English. Perhaps they have always been merchants. Certainly not all the peoples of a Muslim provenance are as friendly to Americans as the man of the corner grocery store is to me. One thinks of the Iraqis and Iranians (although I have known many who hate their governments and love America). One thinks of the Algerians who picked my pocket in Paris. One thinks of the young Pakistanis who are alleged to have blown up the World Trade Center (after having been trained by the C.I.A. to subvert the Russians in Afghanistan). No, we enjoy each other in spite of our origins, not because of them.

One thinks of *A Passage to India*, of Stoppard's *Indian Ink*, of Salman Rushdie.

I have not broached the subject of literature in the store. Who knows what can of worms I might be opening, what box belonging to Pandora.

I moonlight on occasion grading essays on a test of writing skills of those for whom English is a second language. As such I could be regarded as either an opener or a closer of doors. In reality I suppose I am both. I do not agonize over it. It is a good test and everyone connected with it strives to be fair. We do not know whose papers we are grading. The computer can tell if there is bias in our grading. If so, we are no longer invited to grade. The system has every possible guarantee of impartiality built into it. I do my job and cash my paycheck. But I do not mention this avocation in the store. Who knows what relative may recently have been notified of a low score on this particular test. Some things are better left unsaid.

What we do banter about is the Lottery. I say, "I think I'm getting closer to winning."
"Tonight's jackpot is forty million."

"Maybe I'd better wait a week. I'm not sure that I could retire on forty million."
"What will you do with all your money when you win?"
"I'll probably spend most of it on Diet Pepsi."
He laughs: "You'll be able to buy the Pepsi company."
"I wish I'd bought a little bit of it a long time ago."
"Yes, Coke and Pepsi are all over the world."
"Their only war is with each other."
"And maybe even then they share the pie."
"It's a big pie. Enough for both."
"Oh well, good luck; I hope you win."
"I hope if I don't win that you do."
I mean it. I give him the thumbs up. He returns the gesture, seems to get a kick out of doing something so American. At that moment we are the Ebert and Siskel of Existence, giving two thumbs up to Life, its agonies and ecstacies and simple exigencies.

I had to quit eating Kellogg's Raisin Bran. A little too much fiber. I was getting cramps. The boxes sat on the shelf. The expiration date passed. No one else was buying them. I brought a couple of boxes home anyway. Tried to interest my kids in a healthier breakfast. They ridiculed that notion as they poured milk on their Captain Crunch. I gave the Raisin Bran another try myself. In a few days I was taking Immodium-D. The Kellogg's Raisin Bran remained stacked high and wide in the store. I tried not to glance in that direction on my way to the Diet Pepsi coolers.

The diet drinks, on the other hand, began to sell out. I seemed to have started something. He couldn't keep them in stock. He did not have a high priority with the distributors. I suspected him of going to his competitors to put a few liters on his shelves for me. He said, "You are such a good customer--you keep coming in even though so often I am out of what you like."

"It's no big deal," I said. "What you don't have today, I'm
sure you'll have tomorrow."

"You are my best customer," he said.

I said, "Just a second--I'm forgetting something."

I went back for a box of Kellogg's Raisin Bran, a half-gallon of
bluish skim milk, and a package of Immodium-D.

I don't know how well or badly that the store is doing. I tend
to go in it off-hours, mid-morning, mid-afternoon. I haven't
noticed any tell-tale signs yet, such as shrinking inventory. It's
still pretty much a two-person operation. For a while there
was an attempt to sell sandwiches, but that didn't pan out.
My friend does not show worry, but of course he wouldn't. He
would smile and shrug. He would have been through worse.
What worries me is that every store that has ever been in that
location has gone under. There seems an inevitability to such
things. Some locations can't lose; some can't win.

Location, location, location. Like there will always be something strategic about Pittsburgh.

I keep shopping there, even though I know it's stupid. Not the
major shopping--my wife does that at the supermarket. But
the diet drinks, the Lotto tickets, the odds and ends that we
run out of.

I tell myself that time is money, but what kind of money
am I making with the time I save? I tell myself it's nice to
have a place where I can cash a check, but there's an ATM
machine almost as close. I tell myself I've always preferred to
hand over my money to a human being rather than a corpora-
tion. But this way I am handing over more of it.

When I'm a little short on funds, such as at tax-time, I swear
off for a while, but then I miss the place. I even feel a little
guilty. Which is ridiculous: I am my storekeeper's keeper?

I think that I'm just lazy.

This isn't a Big Story. It doesn't have a dramatic conclusion.
No violence, death, betrayal. If there's a theme, you'll have to

find it for me. It's a small part of my life, no doubt an even smaller part of his. As they say in the Mafia, "It's nothing personal, just business."

I don't know why I've even wasted your time, not to mention my own. It's just life.

khan singh kumar
Ealing, England

She Turns Down Her Ticket To The Homeland

"I can't spend Christmas in your snake garden
with spicy food with chilis from jars
packed in like Medusa's head, throttled
by noisy foreigners and all these scaly claimants
worming up to me so they'll get called over
and this sunt - cold as stone: *for dis girl*
vee hab many men to make her vife.
Staying up late,
poised in the mosquito net of a charpoy
for fear a cobra slip in my pyjamas
or first thing in the morning, on a sandy walk
with the snake charmer chaperone
disappeared for tea
and his mongoose done a runner,
caught between sun and terrain
and the songs of hissing from a seeded bed
when the blind come up for air
with a mouthful of scramming ants, behind me -
a stone unturns to a python's wrath,
a python's whipping tongue, foaming
dog who dribbles this way on three legs
with Indian time on my hands
in my Pied-a-terre's, my unprotected skirt
as a sleepy beehive falls from a tree, please
you can keep your air fare
and the fields you think I'll end up sowing
if I live here too long, just lock me with a brochure
in the concrete world
of my clean and pleasant bedroom
waiting for Santa."

sunt - holy man

Catcall

"She was brown before she was white
before she became your wife
she was holding fast her father's contacts, me
and all that lives in her mother's memory.
Enough respect for being stiff lipped
when your legs were on hold
so don't go running your true colours to the football team
in the Fox and Hound, how you love her
for what she is
when we're not the only dejected suitor
sprung from a box. Since the black cat
came between us, we've all been through the pale.
Don't think for a day, we hold it like our parents:
when one of my grandads
cleaning sinks in his first job
had KBW's at the Queen's Building
gob on his red turban, we
went crawling to the temple,
pleading the police. We don't do that again.
These are the black belt streets. There's a custom:
You buy her a bouquet of roses,
who buys the foreplay of bruises?
You take our bride our wives,
we take your pride or lives. Or
put you through the wash. No offence.
We do the same with hindus, jews, muslims,
blacks. We
mean to deal with our own.
You hand her in
to the RSPCA
before it gets too late."

KBW- Keep Britain White

42

When The Social Worker Came Back For More

"I should raise my voice
to give you a taste of the shame.
So stop swirling your G&T
in our pubs
as though your appetite's unabated.
Looking tetchy - mission not concluded yet?
Not met your quota?
Not enough to single out my sister,
upset under a bus shelter;
to bullet point her with incentives;
log her into your networks;
evaluate her with specialists;
with clothes - camouflaged; expecting soon
that the family will surrender to her wishes.
Now she's in the radar,
swept under your auspices,
who from your lot will abet
the agraphobic, paranoidal or schizophrenic
thumb-whirling prayers of the father?"

peter knaggs

Hull, England

Phlegm

I'm stuffing the blanket into my ear,
to muffle the sound of his engine coughing,
heart spluttering, cattarh in his carburettor.
I squeeze my ear into the pillow,
to block out the wheeze of his fan-belt,
to push away the seizing of his lungs,
the slow caul of his lubrication system,
galloping up snotty phlegm,
the feeble spit-spit of it into the bedside mug,
his only mug, I cup it downstairs,
rinse it out, pour tea, add saccharine,
two heaped teaspoonfuls of St Ivel five pints.
One day I'd had enough and stepped the stair-rods
with my father's Valium and morning tea,
and learnt, oil and water don't mix.

Seat Still Warm

Although I start a new job on Monday
there's something perturbing in my replacement,
a lack of respect in the job centre
postcard for a situation not quite vacant.

Something rankles with the recruitment process
curriculum vitae sent through the post
with relevant experience, career ambitions,
just let me question their qualifications,

tinker with the person specification,
reveal certain aspects slightly more telling
like weight, shoe size, inside leg measurement,
musical preferences, football persuasion.

The selected few invited to interview
should hand in dissertations, sit four hour papers
be cross-examined by a twelve person jury
complete an army assault course in under two minutes.

MI5 should be involved at top level
for getting the truth out of referees
of referees forwarding references
of candidates achieving short-list selection.

Under spotlight the interrogation
should be disarming, slightly perplexing,
who scored the fastest ever goal in a world cup?
How many Pogues albums are there in your collection?

The Radio

Recalling my twelfth birthday,
again my dad has no money,
again I am given an empty
birthday card,
he nearly hits me
for being greedy.
"If you want a present,
you can have this".
He points at the wall unit,
a radio cassette player,
a raffle prize.
Before I unplug it he says,
"It's yours, if you want it,
but it stays there."
Until November my brothers
and sisters make tapes
of their favourite hits
in the charts, on my radio-
cassette player.

Then, on my sister's birthday
my dad gives it to her.

Just To Let You Know

There's more fat on me now
than the average greasy chip.

I've managed to go all day without
the slightest desire for a clip round lug hole,

survived eight and twenty years and no one
has made a pair of garters out of my guts.

At lunch time just for the sheer hell of it,
I bought a rice pudding and blew the skin off.

Then I stepped into a wet paper bag
and punched my way out of it.

Believe it or not, I then went to Scarborough
and had a ride on a donkey, with Willie Carson.

Earlier I bought four pieces of two by two,
tapped them together with panel pins,

to frame myself.

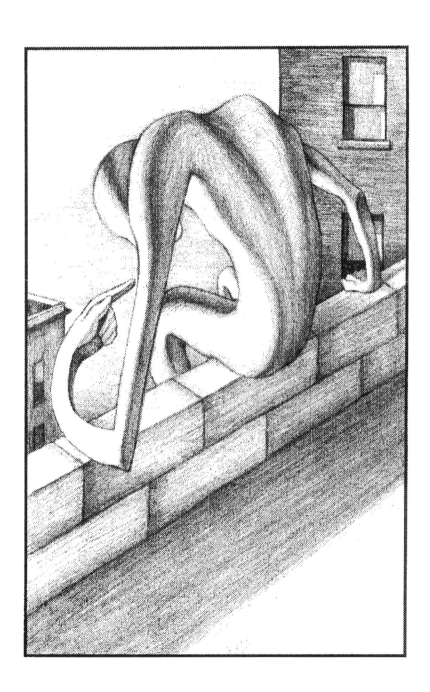

k. m. dersley

Ipswich, England

Them And Their Postures

If only someone got onto prime-time and told it, thought Oxo, laid it all out. The grist to the mill, the cream-offs, the rake-offs. The toss-offs too, for that matter. It had to be falling apart with graft, influence and selfishness, like every other area of the shoddy world. Here was one leather-jacketed type (consciously so, with long, thinning dyed black hair, almost a 'Goth') who knew it. The fact was though that candidly speaking he now formed part of the shit storm himself. He'd got a shot at one area of the seed cake that was small press British poetry. His very own book was going to hit, if not he stands, then a few bedside tables amongst his clan.

A local firm funded by Mervyn Lassiter and with several other amateurs involved was bringing out his fifty-page book of poems called *The Streets of Rome Were Never Like This.*

Oxo's only real involvement with the scene proper was at second hand, through what he heard from Lassiter and Terry Anders. Anders had in effect edited *Streets* for him, transcribing handwritten poems from odd pieces of paper, though some had been word-processed by computer-minded friends. Anders regularised the spelling and cut out some of the imagery; Oxo allowed full licence. After all, Anders and Lassiter actually bought magazines and knew the market. They'd sit down, find a piece of paper, envelope, stamp and cheque and SUBSCRIBE.
Between them they covered a good dozen mags, including *Krox Teeth, Poetry Document* and *Copper Kettle*. Though Oxo took the addresses and sent out poems once or twice he hadn't got anywhere. He'd crack the nut some other way.

What he'd definitely like to see was more of a satirical light thrown on the scene. As in the days of Juvenal, whose work he knew from an American paperback of the poems translated by Hubert Creekmore. The tie between the ancient world (where

he felt entitled to imagine himself a sort of Colossus) and the
States, under whose spell he like so many of his generation
had fallen during many a TV and video and CD hour, seemed
meaningful. The book's title was in honour of the Latin bard.
The implication being that the civilised world had deteriorated
further still from the Rome of the legacy hunters, pseuds,
nouveaux-riches and homos of both sexes.

Lassiter and Anders, who had worked so hard for the locally-
funded and grantless imprint Turtle Press, were also going to
be on hand for the launch of the book at the Star and Sail.
Anders had agreed to act as MC and was lately sporting a
'stylish' goatee that he would salivate into as he lambasted the
punters. His belly seemed a bit bloated these days, and from
the way his white shirt billowed over his gut one Workshop
poet would remark that he resembled the young Sir Peter
Hall.

Apart from a poster or two in the library foyer, which seemed
sensible enough, the methods employed in drawing an
audience were dubious. Lassiter for example went around
playing on Oxo's decadent image. With the right people this
approach worked okay, though one likely candidate was told:
'The boy's a good poet, and not only that, he'll see you're all
right. It's all laid on, if you get me. You know him, don't you?
The bloke with the green teeth and black fingernails? ...You'll
be all right, he's making some sandwiches.

It had been noted often enough by Lassiter, a Supply Teacher,
and Anders, who worked in local government as a Data Input
Assistant, that those who do nothing *can* do nothing, and
those who are doing most are capable of more and more. Oxo,
a good type, was putting effort and elbow grease into his two-
nights-a-week graphics course at the college no doubt, but he'd
been a dole wallah for a solid seven of his twenty-eight years.
And he looked to go on like that forever--or until what he
imagined would be his real money as a poet came in. Even the
house he shared had been chosen with some regard to close-
ness to the DSS office. One thing Oxo had going for him how-

56

air of lovable helplessness that inclined people to line up and offer aid. Lassiter was in effect picking up the tab for Oxo's book, and also paying for the food at his launch party. The £15 required for the single-sided metal tape that would be used to record the event (on a borrowed machine) was put up by someone else--certainly not Oxo.

The night arrived. Anders was glad of the microphone, but swore this would be his last effort as MC. He read one of his own efforts out, but apart from that the thankless task was worth avoiding. You always had to be worrying where other people were. No one gave him credit for his what he imagined to be American barrel-rolling talk: '*Hurry, hurry, hurry!* Friends, put your hands together because tonight we have as you know an all-star bill and I want to call to the bandstand an artist whose work I admire quite a bit.....'

Lassiter had contented himself in the first half with lining up drinks for people that Oxo brought to him in a steady stream, but in the second half he took the stand and orated. Mumbling into his chin, spectacles wobbling and misty, he soon reverted to schoolmaster when there was no respectful hush and bellowed, 'You! *Sit down!*'

The room thinned considerably during his act. Fortunately there was another bar down the corridor.

But Oxo, it could not be denied, was a phenomenon. Anders had never heard such ovations. It wasn't because of the book's merits, in his opinion--while worth publishing, it was a bit derivative--but because people wished to help the feckless Oxo. The boy was quite pitiless too--everybody *had to pay and pay.* Even his grandmother shelled out four quid. His father paid twelve. Not a discount all night. Oxo knew how a star behaved--he seemed bored as he signed flyleaves and casually instructed Anders to open another package of the masterwork.

A number of other poets were present that night to read their things. Oxo was good like that--he didn't mind giving the

others a chance. But then, as Anders noted to himself, these
poets, most of them from the Workshop based at the Lord
Raglan, were calculated to make anyone half-inspired who
took the stand after them look like a god.

When poor Lester, a quiet lad with a talent for pathetic
rhyme, hardly turned a head Anders got emotional and
grabbed the mike.

'All right, we know he hasn't got one of these fancy books out,
but give the bloke a CHANCE--!'

Evangeline, also from the Workshop, sniffed at the book that
was being launched, or *booklet* rather, and said she didn't
have any change on her. 'At least the lines are on straight
this time,' she pointed out to Lassiter with a smirk. 'I think
that's so important, don't you?'

'Not really' he replied. 'The main thing is the quality of the
undying verse.'

By then she was already gathering her own artworks
together to lay before the masses.

She must have been thinking of the previous Turtle Press
booklet, thought Lassiter as he finished a jar of Nero's
Gusset. It was a thing of Anders' called *Pennington Fair*.
The author had typeset it himself on an ancient Imperial,
cutting and pasting the pages together along with some
scrawly bits of artwork executed by his cousin. The result
was supposed to be authentic, or ethnic or something. So far
it had sold twenty-three copies of a run of 500.

Evangeline intoned a couple of her own outpourings, insisting
that neither of them was quite finished. ('Always a mistake,
that,' grunted Anders as he picked up Lassiter's glass
alongside his own and headed for the bar. 'You never
apologise. Act as if they're getting the best right off the top
of the cracker barrel, I tell ya.')

58

Graham Buckingham was from the Workshop as well. Buckingham had a high-powered job, took taxis everywhere, spent long weekends in Munich and Vienna and not only in the course of duty, and he didn't know what a poetry magazine looked like. It was true that he had two or three times put up the money for a *genuine* poet who had a glossy book in a shop to visit Gippeswyk and declaim. But that was so he could collar the bards in question afterwards, male or female, and read a sheaf of his own things. (These were, unfortunately, not totally without merit.) Buckingham spent so much of his time and vital force earning money that the world would have seemed cockeyed to him if there hadn't been a quick way into everything, including the back stairs of poetry, with the help of golden showers.

Strange to say, he wasn't getting anywhere yet, so far as anyone could see, though he sneered at the things Anders and Lassiter sometimes got printed.

It was a cold night of coughs and smoke and peregrinations to and from the other bar, of standing on one leg and listening to the 'literature' and muttering personal observations about the bard to some other mug-cradling satirist. (A proportion of the smoke came from joints, and Anders, who had a horror of virginia as well as all other combustible weeds, kept pointing out that this room was non-smoking. In the end he gave up or he'd have been honorary policeman as well as MC.)

Digusted, Anders abandoned the whole shebang before the end, leaving any readers to introduce themselves. Lassiter saw him go towards the door and pointed at the tables littered with scraps of french toast, peanuts, rolls, cheese straws, pats of butter and pools of cider and lager with disintegrating dog ends and asked, worried-like, 'Who's gonna clean clean up?'

'Find someone,' grunted Anders over his shoulder.

roddy lumsden

London, England

My Realm of the Senses

the liquoricy stink of badger dirt

a mouthful of pig's thinkers, chilled and raw

the cookie-dough complexion of the heart

that you need to be touched just there just so

the spitting sound of burning pigeon-wings

I know I know I shouldn't know such things

My Dark Side

Just as my forebears, every winter,
moving farther north, would grow paler
with a little extra fat marbling their flesh

and just as, after those two summers
I worked the beaches, I could only walk
as if the sand was thick beneath my feet,

so my women always sense a depth,
another side to me I hide from them,
behind the firewall, nurturing its luck.

Drummond

If what you're asking me is if I'm truly sure
It was Drummond that I saw, then let me say it here
And now that no one else has hair like fallow deer
And no one has a forehead like a vintage car,
Nor ears like skating rinks, nor eyes like Ecuador,
Nor teeth like wishing wells, that chin of chicken-wire,
The fortnight nose, a mouth like Milton Keynes on fire,
The smile he borrowed from a passing dinosaur.
For proof though, there's that little matter of the square
Root of minus one he has tattooed somewhere
We ought not mention and the halal abattoir
He smells of and that scrachle of a signature
Which adolescent girls yank up their boob-tubes for.
Believe me, reports of Drummond's death are gossamer.

Scarlet

I think of Bobby Shafto, lost at sea,
his buckles snagged on the wreck in the wrack,
Johnny in the ditch, one scarlet ribbon biting his neck,
who never did make it home from the fair,
Tommy Tucker singing the song of a slashed throat
and Boy Blue, found in the haycock, of whom it was said
he looked for all the world like he was sleeping, not dead.

And I think of my friends and of their friends
and theirs, sitting round the tables in Black Bo's,
not one moral left between them and I suppose
that I must soon finish this and join them,
all the things we know but cannot tell each other
about each other in this half-life of secrets,
the summer night music of now and what-comes-next.

Communion

On the ten mile stretch from Magdala to Omphalos,
they are waiting in droves to gun us down.
We always knew, one day we'd go too far:

that snipy old lady we tarred and feathered,
the little blond boy we robbed and reddened
with wire wool, the hippy vegan girl we force fed

bad meat through a funnel, six days straight;
the canal will cough its secret, one of these long, hot days.
And you know the sentence, for women and children.

You. Of course, I'll always remember you.
As if our love was less noble, less true
because of these few things love made us do.

joan jobe smith

Long Beach, USA

Wired!!

Wired on English tea I brought back
from Yorkshire, not used to drinking
caffeine: I want to cry! I want to sing!
I want to call everyone I love and tell
them I love them, call everyone I hate
and tell them I hate them but would
forgive them if they would love me.
I want to wash the cars, wallpaper
the ceiling, I want to wear purple
and have a party, invite everyone
within a 100-mile radius. I want to
write a screenplay about myself and
award myself the Oscar for Lifetime
Wonderfulness- I want to corporate
takeover Bill Gates, give away his
billions to the homeless and single
mothers (fathers too), I want to track
down my no-good ex-husband, no-good
ex-son-in-law and President Clinton
and tie them to two-legged stools
and hit them on the head with a wet
umbrella till they say "I'm sorry
please forgive me we were fools!" I
want three wishes, one of which to use
to revert my children to infancy for
one minute so I can once again kiss
their sweat-button fingertips, I want
to dance on the rooftop of the highest
hotel in San Francisco and yell to the
world the secret of my mashed potatoes,
I want more English Yorkshire tea !!

Married to the Machinist Poet

Every day poems he writes as diligently as
A rising sun and when he reads them to me
In bed on weekends, at the kitchen table
Workdays his poems about the machine shop
The world at large, sometimes one about me
I always think I just may be the luckiest
Woman alive finally married to my Robert
Browning, Neruda, Shakespeare, Baudelaire.

But then comes the rumors of lay-off and now
Lay-offs and his poems are about the concrete
Emptiness of shop floors the echoes off their
Tin walls, the loneliness of chain cranes and un-
Manned machines when just a year ago Goodstone
Was boasting about becoming a Goldstone with
The mother lodes of billion dollar contracts.

Today when he kissed me goodbye in the dark
5 a.m. his lunchpail in hand his soft beard
Upon my face I lay wondering what his poem
Will say tonight while I wander in our home
Looking for turf and loose coal alongside the
Road, good omen when I drop a knife avert my
Eyes hoping it does not point my way and if it
Does, kick it to spin it, pretend I didn't see.

Mack the Maniac

Just out of prison for manslaughter, six-
and-a-half-foot tall 300-pound Mack the
Maniac started coming around my daughter
wanting his $500 back my son-in-law'd
ripped off Mack the Maniac in a gone-wrong
crack scam Mack the Maniac yelling gimme
back my money or I'll rip your head off
and my son-in-law said tomorrow tomorrow
but tomorrow when Mack the Maniac came back
my son-in-law climbed out the bathroom window
to go hide in a beer bar so Mack the Maniac
yelled at my daughter gimme my money gimme
my money and she said next week next week
and when next week came Mack the Maniac
kicked down the door but my son-in-law was
still gone and the next day Mack the Maniac
left a note written in blood: Gimme my money
or else! so my daughter called the cops who
said there wasn't anything they could do
even though Mack the Maniac kept coming
around while my son-in-law kept staying away
and pretty soon Mack the Maniac got a crush
on my daughter felt sorry for her for having
such an asshole for a husband and pretty soon
Mack the Maniac began leaving rosebuds on her
porch and she became very afraid so one day
when I was there and Mack the Maniac came
to the door I yelled up at him: If you don't
leave my daughter alone I will rip off your
head and Mack the Maniac looked down at me
one-third his size his haircut slashing at
the doorjamb and he laughed and said: Little
Lady, I bet you would. And Mack the Maniac
never came around again so my son-in-law

came home again strutted around saying how
he'd run off Mack the Maniac had scared the
SHIT out of Mack the Maniac and how I wished
I'd let Mack the Maniac that good fine man
rip my son-in-law's head off and use it for
a bowling ball while I'd had the chance.

Poem from the Los Angeles County Gaol

Yes I went to jail one night although
I was innocent just like those other
women there bamboozled by some man:
the young bleached blonde from Utah
who snuck out her bedroom window to
date the boy her father hated and rode
passenger in his stolen car all the way
to California; the middle-aged lady
facing 10 counts of Murder One for
performing abortions for money to pay
her husband's gambling debts because
she loved him so; the grey-haired widow
who sat on her cot hands folded school
girl ashamed for shoplifting to get by
after her husband of 40 years suddenly
died leaving her with nothing, all of
them women just like you or your mother
with ovaries, eyebrows, toes, women
with over the rainbow dreams, oh, and
those 20 biker chicks busted with their
biker old men after holding an entire
town hostage for a weekend of brawl,
the next day the biker chicks when we
all put back on our own clothes to go
for arraignment in court angry when
they saw they'd been laundered: dammit,
said the one who liked to have the most
fun riding holding tight onto her tough
leather biker old man thinking fun is
wind blowing in your hair, something
hard between your legs (and maybe it is).
Dammit, she said, they washed away all
my old man's pecker tracks. Do any of
you know how long it took us to do that?
I didn't want to know. I was innocent.

labi siffre
Abergavenny, Wales

Economomedy 2

I saw   a small   Kampuchean girl
Aged seven   or six   sifting through filth
on a rubbish tip   close to Phnom Penh
for tins   and rags
to sell   for a few riels

And I didn't know what to do

So I took my cheque book   and ripped one out
and I wrote a cheque   for a hundred pounds
and posted it   to a charity org   for street kids and orphans
in far away places

but I felt no better   and that's alright   'cause who am I trying
to help?

I saw a small Kampuchean   girl   of seven or six
sifting through filth   on a rubbish tip close to Phnom Penh
for tins and rags   to sell   for a few riels   or sen

And I didn't know what to do

So I took some paper   and a pencil   and wrote
some poems   about her plight   and my fight
to make myself feel   like I'm doing my best
or at least   "the least I can do"   to help

and I read the poems   at a reading   and
the audience was moved   they really liked
my poems   and word   went around   and folk
came around   to hear me read my   "Cambodian Suite"

and the beat goes on
and I'm grateful   because
that girl   is paying   my rent

Mantra

I need this job I have kids I'm doing this
for my children besides everyone else
does it if we don't someone else will we
can't take unilateral action in the
national interest a level playing field is
what we want if everyone else stops we
can anyway what difference will it make
your being simplistic fascistic idealistic
oh yes very sixties politically correct
chattering classes one person can't
make a difference this is the real world
be practical pragmatic realistic you
have no monopoly of compassion what
difference will it make get off the cross
someone else needs the wood charity
begins at home besides I need this job I
have kids I'm doing this for my children

Benediction

More than anything I've dreamed
awake or sleeping   heartspeak U
be making me suffer

knives electric shocks and hammers
My head is ringing my life sings
Hallel Hallel but there ain't no U-Jah

the truth, what is? (the least) no fool ya
The beast is in my eyes   I fear to lose ya
The beast is in my eyes   I'm yours complete

that's how I rule ya   The beast is in my eyes
your hands deciding this or that thrill
to play how my body sway

Your life invades my flesh
you really do take my breath away
The cynic on parade in me says.. "a day a week

a year at most   then one throw the other away"
The child who battles every day and will forever know
I *don't* believe, insists you are The Host

I take you to my tongue   the congregation sneer
their fear... you are The Host   the bells are rung
I take you to my tongue and wash

your eyes   your lips   your neck   your chest
your arms and belly   thighs and feet and then
your cock until you gasp and gurgle   softly into sleep

lisa glatt

Long Beach, USA

My Sweetest Piece

On a Sunday in June, my stepfather stood in the backyard. At the picnic table, he balanced a watermelon on its side. He held a large knife. My mother stood beside him in a floral dress and white sandals. She was eating a hard boiled egg. Every now and then she lifted the salt shaker above her egg, then took a little bite. It was the first day I'd worn a bra, and I remember my mother teasing me, saying, *Look at her new breasts, perky, like mine.*

My stepfather looked from the watermelon to my new breasts and nodded. He sliced it into pieces. The melon bled onto the table. *When I was a boy in Jordan*, my stepfather began, slicing while he talked, *was special, and my parents knew it, and they had...* and then he looked at my mother, searching for a word. My mother shrugged, popped the last of the egg in her mouth. *Well*, he continued, *they had a tool, it was a knife in that it was very sharp, but it was long and round and hollow, sharp – what do you say.' Cylinder, that's it,. My mother would hold the watermelon up on its eye, lengthwise, balance it for my father, who would use the cylinder to extract the middle, that long, sweet piece, for me – the boy.*

But he wasn't a boy now, he was a man, and he wasn't in Jordan, but in a California suburb. It was 1975. It was the early a.m. I was walking toward the bathroom. And when he found me in the hall, he muttered something to my new body, then rubbed his swollen tongue over my lips. I understood I was red. I understood I was juicy. My stepfather took a cylinder from his pocket. He drilled and drilled, until he had it – all that he was so entitled to, all of me that was sweet.

The Atheist's Tunnel

A woman in a bright yellow coat wraps the cuff around my arm
and asks me first about headaches, and then about cramps, and
then about my mother, dead early from breast cancer, which
makes me just a tad more interesting than the young women
here whose mothers are still breathing. It's my first visit since
she died, and the woman wants to know how I feel, do I feel OK.
She remembers I lived with my mother while I wrote and nursed
at once. *I didn't nurse, I say, I was a miserable bitch in the next
room, I was what my mother called a bummer*, but she's not
listening anymore, this cheerful woman dressed up like a flower.
She's leading me into the examining room, where teddy bears and
buttercups line the walls, where a three foot picture of Santa
hangs even though it's April. I'm in that paper robe, leaning back
into position, wondering about Santa's perseverance when the
doctor enters. He wants to know my mother's age, which breast,
and I'm surprised when I say left, not because I know it, but
because it's there on my tongue, and then I'm moving towards
him, and I'm thinking that it's a wonderful thing my love and I
don't have sex on a table like this, that he doesn't see me in this
light, that he doesn't peer in with sticks and tools. Just then the
doctor pipes up, saying my cervix looks great, and he says this
with such enthusiasm that I suddenly see my cervix made up for
the prom, lipstick and blush, a pink glow that speaks of health
and well being. He wants to talk about life and death, about
heaven, and I'm wincing, not because the speculum is cold, but
because I know how unpopular my beliefs are, even here among
these scientists, so I say nothing as the doctor chatters on about
his own dead mother. *Oh I understand how you feel. I was just
thirty when my mother died, but I believe in God, you must
believe in God, you do believe in God?* he says, his head popping
up from between my knees, and l see him, a believer in latex
gloves, a balding orphan in bright light. I force a smile and he
returns to my crotch. *You must believe in heaven*, he continues,

at it. *I'm certain that when mama went she went into a tunnel, a beautiful tunnel*, he says, at the exact moment his finger is scooting into my ass.

Spaz

My stepfather, Ahmad, was an enthusiastic nudist and sex
therapist, a zealot who believed sexual repression made one ill,
that the *orgasm* could cure everything – the sick way he felt
about himself, my mother's arthritis, his little brother's
epilepsy. He flew the boy to America. It was 1975. I was twelve
with tiny breasts, my heart a new, flipping thing; I was ready
to love the first boy off the plane, regardless of his condition.
But Zeod arrived in September with his uneven breathing and
a permanent snarl. Only fifteen, he had a full beard and wore
slacks, which convinced me early on that he was no potential
boyfriend. And once I realized that Zeod wasn't my future
husband I joined my brother in laughing behind his back.
Spaz, we called him. *When's he going to spaz*, we wondered
out loud.

My parents took Zeod to UCLA Medical Center, drove him to
San Francisco for the weekend, checking out Stanford, up and
down the coast, stopping at the world's best hospitals. No one
could promise a cure. In October Ahmad sat his brother down.
He explained that he alone could control his disease. Ahmad
promised that if the boy came often enough, freely, without
inhibition, the seizures would stop.

Zeod loved my stepfather's suggested medicine, took to
masturbating everyday, all hours of the day and night, sitting,
stroking, curing himself in every room of our suburban home.

One Friday I returned from school and found him on the
couch, going at it. He shrugged, waved me away, and I'd felt
his irritation – it wasn't that I'd caught him doing something
private, but more like I'd interrupted his favorite TV show.

Weeks went by and Zeod didn't spaz, not when he was tired or hungry, not even when he came down with the flu. Ahmad was thrilled, insisting it was worth it – each embarrassing moment and extra load of laundry. It started to make sense to my mother, brother, and me. My brother and I stopped laughing. We stopped waiting. We were a family who believed in the orgasm, who'd witnessed its power.

No one understood why two months later, while sitting in a Jack-in-the-Box, holding a dripping burger in his hand, Zeod started to shake, the burger falling into his now quaking lap, the terrible sounds coming from his throat and chest and somewhere deeper, no one understood his flailing hands and jerking shoulders. And we were all let down, the five of us who believed for months in the orgasm, who'd hoped it would save our lives.

carol coiffait
Welton, England

Monsieur Magritte Berates The Beatles

You know, you failed to sing
about Eleanor Rigby's other bits;
like her night-shift
with the built-in plastic tits
that she'd slip into on a Saturday night
to confuse her Father.

Also, you neglect to mention
in that particular song,
that once, she did leave home.
(Where she was all but invisible)
But not for very long
about a month, I think.

Before she left, she stuck
her Mother's favourite shoes,
the ones with built-in bunions,
onto the kitchen table
for bad luck.

Then she stitched the hem up
on that shift, closed it like a bag
and stuffed it full of vegetables and rice
and hung it in the hall
close to the telephone.

Her parents didn't notice
that she'd gone, until one night
her Father accused her of sulking
and of being pregnant.
He said that she did right to hang
her head in shame.

Her Mother blamed her for
spending too long
on the 'phone...

When at last she did come home,
smirking round the kitchen door,
she cooked and cleaned for them
for thirty years or more
and saw them safely
to their grave.

Then you people got it right;
she lived alone to dry, old age.

Short Cut No. 1

Involves a razor-blade or gun:
A messy way to join you, son.

Short Cut No.2

Involves a pair of specs., the latest book
A pot of tea or coffee and a fag.

These things assist the electricity
To turn inwards, soothe two damaged hearts

The toilet's privacy an added bonus
Until memory is pulled in
On a stretched tendon to tear us apart.

Still, I am comforted, strong enough
To carry on, despite my thigh-bone's twitch
Tap, tapping out its latest message
To mobility on an old tin drum.

Once, I believed that love alone
Would guarantee a virus-free seed.
Indeed, the first-fruits were wonderful
But didn't keep too well,
Just three decades.

Hell... Who am I kidding.
The fastest short-cut
Back to you involves
A spade.

Dog Story

A bitch on heat is worth a bar
of chocolate or a can of condensed milk.

A male pup is worth nothing
until the telephone rings.

A female pup could get you
into serious trouble.

At six weeks, the whole litter
could provide a marriage portion

A feast for the whole village, or
a new set of floats for the head-man.

Weaned, they could make your fortune
or take you to an early grave.

But one thing is certain,
when that bitch is old enough to breed

She could bring down the government
with her lickspittle tongue.

tricia cherin
Long Beach, USA

Grand Central Station

There you were in D.C.
after all day at the Library of Congress
relaxing at Barbara Smith's place on Saturday night
listening to a great little combo
with your daughter Eva
well-named for primal woman
and for knightly battles,
yours not least.

You called me from the pay phone
to note the arrivals and departures
to tell me about the Romanesque architecture
and to wish I were there.

Did you wake up that morning and say to yourself,
Today I must place myself in a
site of great metaphoric possibility.

Meaning Making

Coverage models are out of favor
in hermeneutics and housekeeping.
I will never organize the top floor right
or know HOW TO KNOW for more than recess.

We've settled for accommodations,
for doings in contexts,
for incremental finitudes.

I like a certain thoroughness
in considerations gathered,
a repertoire of ironies
in the jewelry box,
but I know now
there is no done.

Better to clatter
the rattles of ourselves,
HEAR ourselves,
a cacophonous signification.

charles bukowski

(1920-1994) Los Angeles, USA

(Bukowski's first ever published interview)
Chicago Literary Times, March 1963

CHARLES BUKOWSKI SPEAKS OUT

By Arnold L. Kaye, Los Angeles Correspondent.

To the interviewer, Charles Bukowski is as the yeti to the Himalayan explorer. He's hard to find and when you've found him, life becomes exceedingly dangerous. It has been said by some, that there is no Charles Bukowski. A persistent rumor for many years declared that those gusty poems signed with his name were actually written by a nasty old lady with hairy armpits.

But yes, there is a Charles Bukowski, existing solitarily in a one-room, murphy-bed (yes, cold water) apartment in the heart of Hollywood, shadowed on one side by the Bureau of Public Assistance, Old Age Security Office, and on the other by the Kaiser Foundation Hospital. Poor Charles Bukowski, looking like a retired junkie, seems to belong there.

When he answered the door his sad eyes, weary voice and silk dressing gown told me that here was, in more ways than one, a tired man. We sat and talked, drank beer and scotch, and Charles finally, like a surrendering virgin, gave in to his first interview. From the window, if you stick your head out far enough, you can see the lights in Aldous Huxley's house up the hill, where the successful live.

KAYE: Does it bother you that Huxley is in a position to spit on you?

BUKOWSKI: Oh, that is a good question. [He dived into the recess behind the murphy-bed and came out with a couple of pictures of himself]

KAYE: Who took these?

BUKOWSKI: My girlfriend. She died last year. What was the question?

KAYE: Does it bother you that Huxley is in a position to spit on you?

BUKOWSKI: I haven't even thought of Huxley, but now that you mention it, no, it doesn't bother me.

KAYE: When did you start to write?

BUKOWSKI: When I was 35. Figuring the average poet starts at 16, I am 23.

KAYE: It has been observed by a number of critics that your work is frankly autobiographical. Would you care to comment on that?

BUKOWSKI: Almost all. Ninety-nine out of a hundred, if I have written a hundred. The other one was dreamed up. I was never in the Belgian Congo.

KAYE: I would like to make reference to a particular poem in your most recent book, *Run With the Hunted*. Would you happen to have the name and present whereabouts of the girl you mentioned in 'A Minor Impulse to Complain'?

BUKOWSKI: No. This is no particular girl; this is a composite girl, beautiful, nylon leg, not-quite-whore, creature of the half-drunken night. But she really exists, though not by single name.

KAYE: Isn't that ungrammatical? There seems to be a tendency to classify you as the elder statesman of poet-recluses.

BUKOWSKI:. I can't think of any poet-recluses outside of one dead Jeffers. [Robinson Jeffers] The rest of them want to slobber over each other and hug each other. It appears to me that I am the last of the poet-recluses.

KAYE: Why don't you like people?

BUKOWSKI: Who does like people? You show me him and I'll show you why I don't like people. Period. Meanwhile, I have got to have another beer. [He slouched off into the tiny kitchen and I yelled my next question to him].

KAYE: This is a corny question. Who is the greatest living poet?

108

BUKOWSKI: That is not corny. That is tough. Well, we have Ezra...Pound, and we have T.S.,[Eliot] but they've both stopped writing. Of the producing poets, I would say...Oh, Larry Eigner.

KAYE: Really?

BUKOWSKI: Yeah. I know no one has ever said that. That is about all I can come up with.

KAYE: What do you think of homosexual poets?

BUKOWSKI: Homosexuals are delicate and bad poetry is delicate and Ginsberg turned the tables by making homosexual poetry strong poetry, almost manly poetry; but in the long run, the homo will remain the homo and not the poet.

KAYE: To get down to more serious matters, what influence do you feel Mickey Mouse has had on the American imagination?

BUKOWSKI: Tough. Tough, indeed. I would say that Mickey Mouse had a greater influence on the American public than Shakespeare, Milton, Dante, Rabelais, Shostakovich, Lenin, and/or Van Gogh. Which say "What?" about the American public. Disneyland remains the central attraction of Southern California, but the graveyard remains our reality.

KAYE: How do you like writing in Los Angeles?

BUKOWSKI: It doesn't matter where you write so long as you have the walls, typewriter, paper, beer. You can write out of a volcano pit. Say, do you think I could get 20 poets to chip in a buck a week to keep me out of jail?

KAYE: How many times have you been arrested?

BUKOWSKI: How do I know? Not too many; 14-15 maybe. I thought I was tougher than that but each time they put me in it tears my gut, I don't know why.

KAYE: Bukowski, what do you see for the future now that everybody wants to publish Bukowski?

BUKOWSKI: I used to lay drunk in alleys and I probably will again. Bukowski, who is he? I read about Bukowski and it doesn't seem like anything to do with me. Do you understand?

KAYE: What influence has alcohol had on your work?

BUKOWSKI: Hmm, I don't think I have written a poem when I was completely sober. But I have written a few good ones or a few bad ones under the hammer of a black hang-over when I didn't know whether another drink or a blade would be the best thing.

KAYE: You look a bit under the weather today.

BUKOWSKI: I am, yes. This is Sunday evening. It was a tough eight race card. I was 103 ahead at the end of 7. Fifty to win on the eighth. Beaten half a length by a 60-1 shot who should have been canned for cat food years ago, the dog. Anyway, a day of minor profit or prophet led to a night of drunkenness. Awaked by this interviewer. And I'm really going to have to get drunk after you leave, and I'm serious.

KAYE: Mr Bukowski, do you think we'll all be blown up soon'?

BUKOWSKI: Yes, I think we will. It is a simple case of mathematics. You get the potential, and then you get the human mind. Somewhere down the line eventually there is going to be a damn fool or madman in power who is simply going to blow us all quite to hell. That's all, it figures.

KAYE: And what do you think is the role of the poet in this world-mess?

BUKOWSKI: I don't like the way that question is phrased.

The role of the poet is almost nothing...drearily nothing. And when he steps outside of his boots and tries to get tough as our dear Ezra [Pound] did, he will get his pink little ass slapped. The poet, as a rule, is a half-man – a sissy, not a real person, and he is in no shape to lead real men in matters of blood, or courage. I know these things are anti to you, but I have got to tell you what I think. If you ask questions you have got to get answers.

KAYE: Do you?

BUKOWSKI: Well, I don't know...

KAYE: I mean in a more universal sense. Do you have to get answers?

BUKOWSKI: No, of course not. In a more universal sense, we only get one thing. You know...a head stone if we're lucky; if not, green grass.

KAYE: So do we abandon ship or hope altogether?

BUKOWSKI: Why these clichés, platitudes? OK, well, I would say no. We do not abandon ship. I say, as corny as it may sound, through the strength and spirit and fire and dare and gamble of a few men in a few ways we can save the carcass of humanity from drowning. No light goes out until it goes out. Let's fight as men, not rats. Period. No further addition.

NOTE by Jules Smith

This was Bukowski's first-ever published interview, which hasn't been reprinted since its appearance during March 1963. Its chief fascination now is that it reflects Bukowski before the years of fame and notoriety, but at a turning point in his career. Jon Edgar Webb's magazine *The Outsider* devoted a special issue to Bukowski, and his Loujon Press published the first full-length poetry collection, *It Catches My Heart In Its Hands*, within the same year. At the time of the interview, Bukowski's reputation was very much confined to the readers of little magazines throughout the States. He was the author of only three poetry chapbooks, the most recent being the 32 page *Run With the Hunted*, from R.R. Cuscaden's Chicago-based magazine *Midwest*. It is a reasonable supposition that Cuscaden, one of the earliest and best critical champions of Bukowski's work, may have arranged this interview with the *Chicago Literary Times*. Notwithstanding the several 'politically incorrect' comments - much more glaring today than in 1963, of course -the interview shows a more thoughtful and literary character than Bukowski's later pronouncements allowed, though his attitude towards death, alcohol, racetracks and humanity remained fairly consistent. His best work, arguably from the late 1960s to the late 1980s, lay ahead of him, but in 1963 Charles Bukowski was already forming a distinctive self-image in his readers' minds.

112

sean burn

Newcastle, England

16:X

we've just been 3 hours on th camino real *
me & kilroy & tennessee williams
& now ahm cryin by th monument
as window undressers roll home
& someone walks past shoutin
& someone flicks a lighter
tho they dont smoke
& someone panhandles
& ahm guilty of th apple muffin
warmin ma pocket
knowin they need food
& knowin booze will win
wait til shes gone & aa eat it quickly
fingers all sticky crumbs become evidence
tho all aa hear is *america here is thy son*
& all anyone else hears
r cries of *chronicle* & seagulls
& in th pizza express they dont hear that
only see mouths openin
like so many toppings
& streetlights r gold
gainst honeyed sandstone
& it chimes 5:30 5:45 6 o clock
& this guy sits down
headphones large as tennessee
all tickin & clickin & buzzin & achin
til he hits the rewind & a white stick
hits th chewin gum & no one gives a hand
& ahm on dopiethin & aahm debatin
chuckin ma dole on tequila or scotch
& a bouncer walks past
all aftershave & no neck
& his carrierbag busts & he whispers *ohfuck*
looks round guilty t see if others heard
as sirens a semitone out

& half a beat out wail past without stoppin
& headphones does a runner
past f c u k wich is openin soon
& lynsey & d c & 1 a wz here
& kilroy came saw & wz conquered
& *america here is thy son*
eyesdown crowd searchin for small change
aa listen t their symphonies of feet
down grey streets t th river t th sea
& a wean tugs his father who chills
t 2 men tradin licks on a single 99
& kilroy rises says he is lost & aahm too
& th disorientate ask for directions
t th *demolition in progress*
& a flowerseller packs up her stock
& a woman passes arm round her son
& another mother passes
holdin hands with her child
& aa wish aa cd ask wat all this feels like
cos aa dont know & neither does kilroy
& no one asks *why yu cryin*
tho aa wait for raised hands
& *stopcryin* but aa cant
& as 6:30 sounds
theyre takin it out on kilroy
on his gold boxin gloves theyre chantin
england*america here is thy son*
& th clarinet starts on gershwin in paris
& ahm havin difficulty readin th writin
& kilroy holds out his hat says
aa wz sincere t th camera goin off
weegee in newcastle in pools of blood
not makin front pages & security checks out
2 girls passin arm in armin
& its too cold for shorts short skirts
& ahm cold in a world of anothers makin
where a drunk bellows & kilroy follows
th homeless takin turns

combin their hair
as valpolicella clots
& th temperature drops
& th bouncer returns
holdin hands with his lover
neath anarchies of starlings patchin th sky
still aa hear th cry *here is thy son*
& a guy lets his bouquet slip
t th feet of this platinum bombshell
who's cheered on by toonarmy
into cuttin up biblethumpers
skirt rides up reveals th unmistakeable
tranny with fuckin attitude
& none of em knows wich way t take it
as a girl & her daa bite into whoppas
steam risin off week old cattle
& snakeboarders domino th street
& someone adjusts their laces
pulls on their bonnet
asks if ahm from th church
asks if ahm th preacher
& aa laugh out loud

here is thy son

* kilroy is the lead character in *camino real* – a play
by tennessee williams

trans pennine

        in an age ov double glazin
defenestration becomes twice az hard
& yu ma love had twice az far t fall
than most az aa recall wile speedin
th A66 wich is no route 66 but a more
concrete affair fast trackin east
blurrin fields ov rape wich were not
there then tho their yellow subtext wz

way back wen aa fell for yu yr
hi heel beat & in that stiletto moment
ov waitin on yu choosin *scifi silver*
saw how well yu hid yr difference
& just how subtle yr makeup wz no
red crimes pinned t us az aa palmed
painted dreams small as detonators
across t yu security never workin
where it went nor th wolfwhistlin lads

                   & after
retirin t that caff off th main drag
where they remembered yr makeup
asked who th lucky man wz & refused
payment for our chinese tea smoky
az stolen pearl aa painted on nails
wich yu dug in ma flesh az aa pulled
yu ever tighter onto me mashin lips
like overripe cherries brushin cerise
tart from yr mouth we screwed yu
wisperin how yu never wd never cd
make it az a bloke

                then rackin up
more ov their infamous patisserie
stuffed with all manner ov mango

strawberry peach before dancin out
& across tombstones where we laid
wite crumbs for birds across graffiti

aa wiped a deeper red off yr mouth
wishin t pour th breth back in

even now tastin yr sweetness
th snake upon ma lips

devreaux baker

Mendocino, USA

Nights And The North Sea

With one hour of light left, I walked the two flights to your room.
We have only this dialect of memory we struggle to master.
I sleep with a piece of the Berlin Wall beneath my bed
you say, reaching below to pull up the jagged rock.

Look, the light is leaving, we don't have time for promises
or threats. The woman next door is calling her children in.
On the horizon, one dory waits for the coming night
to translate her shape into something mythic.

I sit, struck speechless with the new moon's features
trapped in all your windows like a prisoner of glass,
squeezing the shape of another country's past
inside my palm,

as though the pressure of flesh alone
could save us from our unknowns.

All the right words wait on the tip of my tongue,
but I'm afraid to say them, and listen instead to the voice
that rises from the bedside radio,
prayers in Latin and in Gaelic,
hopeful and full of trust.

Homesick

You dreamed the bodies of your grandparents
pried out of sleep. Like pieces of a puzzle
they wandered the cool dark range of your body
lonely as two lights at the edge of a marsh.

He carried roses and she carried bread
as gifts for the living. Lifted out of your body
like a pair of hands, fingers mated knuckle to knuckle.

Beneath their feet, war was growing a bitter root
they kept bending to eat. The empty places
their bodies left behind, like chalk circles in a street

got filled with fire, branding the words, Dublin and Belfast,
where you saw a sister calling her lost brother.
Her words like a riddle ricochet through you.

You walk through this house of sleep, turning on lights
so lost shapes rise unharmed by death
until the voice of the radio drops its lifeline
and you grab hold, to rise like the aftermath of a storm,

surrounded by disaster, remembering
the frantic chase of thunder, the sharp thrusts
of lightning, the left behind voices
bleeding right through you.

Myself Greets You

Our first night in New York
we got drunk in Harry's Bar,
you flirted with the Italian bus boy
and fell down the stairs
on the way to the rest room.
But before that we walked for miles
up streets I forget the names of,
so you could photograph the way
the tops of the buildings
cut up the sky.
The truth of that trip is, that I fell in love with you
all over again, a miraculous kind of
rediscovery story,
and if I'm really honest about what happened
I can say it was almost as hard as giving birth,
the way I kept struggling to control you
and the way you kept pushing
to get out.
Until by the time we reached New York
there was nothing left for either one of us to do
but accept that we were bound up one with the other
as something more than mother and daughter.

I kept wanting to say I am just a body
with this crazy ghost wandering through
the endless rooms,
and you are like the voice on the other side
of any disaster,
who talks the survivors through
so they can hang onto that thread of life
until the ambulance arrives and carries them off,
buckled up to some stiff unyielding hospital room board
where you know as they close the doors
and you stand watching,
while the thing roars away sirens blazing,
that thanks to you,
they are going to pull through.

Learning How To Dance

For D.H.

I guess all those mornings my soul fled
afraid to face the body she had worn the night before
I could have told you how much your
gravel-throated voice meant to me

the gentle tugging that so many times
pulled me up
to the surface of my bed
was from some song you played

so we could wake to a name like Louis
stringing words about somebody called Mack
the Knife and the importance of following love
no matter where *you gotta go.*

As for me, I am past falling in love
with strangers on park benches
and past feeling sorry when no one recognizes
the lonely as copper parts of my soul.

This is the Year of the Tiger
and I am going to get strong
no more bourbon in coffee
at dawn.

I might spend the entire winter
in this room
and be perfectly happy
no one knocks at this door.

This might be the beginning place
I've been looking for,
following the thread of a song

128

from out of my own pitch-black place
into the light of what there is
living all around me.

I never knew how close from there to here was,
but I can remember like yesterday
learning how to dance, on the tops of your shoes.

jules smith
Hull, England

The Man Who Shot Simon Armitage

Imagine a Jeremy Paxman "Yee-rrr-ssss?"
Not everyone knows just how it was
that I, of all meek poets, 'went to work'
on Simon Armitage, and wound up here.
I am, because of him, an assassin;
in fact, intention, and in pulp fiction.
Why do such a thing? Well, why does a mere
dog lick its own bollocks? Because it can.
Before embracing the Stygian dark,
I'll explain my Armitigian mark.

Think back to *The Old Poetry* days,
before the Po Biz turned into a craze.
Student Simon, sad, homesick in Portsmouth,
turned his study of violent stuff
into an ambition for verse. Perverse!
He stood in bookshops, turning pages,
relishing Hughes' killer images.
Huddersfield, not Hampstead. This, deeper than
geography, was significance. The man,
that rare bookchap with a liking for Gunn,

was not just another bimbo. The son
shining from under Hattersley's *Wide Skirt*
blinded all of us in *The North* (that squirt
off of bigshot Batman Sansom's old block).
Not just a chapbook poet shouting, cock-
happy; he was cool, calm, and selected,
the smart money on him. As expected,
he rose like a market without a crash;
the smart sober poet and no re-hash.
That brass-tacky cleverness, that action.

I followed his full life and half rhymes.
"A probation officer in Oldham

who versifies between cases" *(The Times)*.
Check out that guy Armitage, I told 'em,
he's the business. Not trying, succeeding.
I had stalked him through many a reading
in Hull, Leeds Waterstones, the South Bank,
whilst thinking up rhymes for J. Arthur Rank.
We were the same age, give or take 6 years.
What was that title – *Distances between Beers?*

Then the 80s gave way to 'The Numties'.
He was shot to prominence. Form Captain
of the New School, the lads, the Young Turkeys
with witty scripts and lots of male action.
Chatto's chap, Faber's populist Poet
for Our Times, and for our football half-times.
He was Boss, and let everyone know it;
to *Verse's* flat dough, he'd added fresh yeast,
and made serious bread. We're talking crimes...
I admired him too much for my own peace.

His exactness and imaginative stretch
enraptured some, made others retch.
Radio One: "check it – this iz Sarmon".
Radio Two: "Today's guest is one
of The New Generation. No, not a dancer..."
Radio Three: "And that was *'Die Ansürre'*
by Schoenberg. Now, Simon Armitage".
Radio Four: "That ends 'Of Human Bondage'.
Presenting the new series of 'Stanza', here's..."
Radio Five Live Simon. Weasel cheers.

It's clear success makes one a target.
I think I know my duty when I see it.
The clincher: National Poetry Day,
after which Something Had To Be Done. For kicks.
Veteran performer at 36,
with 8 books out and one on the way;
our moderne Wystan. (Some said Great White Dope -

not me). I could see his ubiquity
stretching well into the next century,
a dribbling Laureate selling soft soap.

To preserve the glory of his great start
was sacred duty. I must play my part.
Most poets think security means bed.
No 'security consciousness'. Yet if I said
he was blind to danger, that's an untruth.
Simon used to put on a laurel wreath
which would, he supposed, make him lightning-proof.
He had it all, except for levity.
Yet knew it would turn up eventually,
his bête noire, like Bunter's postal order.

Here it comes, beyond the Yorkshire border.
Scene: New Year's Eve, the Millennium Dome.
Icons not built in a day. Simon. Rome.
And here he is: entrance like a boxer,
as seen in the pages of *Vogue, Esquire.*
Mr Black: jeans, polo, leather jacket,
and an earring. Must have cost a packet.
I wore an overcoat, deep of pocket;
a marginal figure, eccentric fan,
like Valerie Solanas, Mark Chapman.

He was a lean man, canny and waddish.
He read in that emphatic style of his
for the last time, professionally surly,
thinking, as always, of leaving early,
of signing books and pocketing the cheque.
He was hypnotic - *hypnos*, from the Greek
for sleep. Yet the audience didn't doze.
"I don't know much about footy or clothes",
said fit young half-Aussie 'Koala' Claire,
"but I liked the one about Cantona".

He was talking Hughes, Shakespeare, the Main Men.
Then seemed to half recognize...Robinson?

And couldn't run away. He was hobbl'n
at the time from a bad back condition.
I said, "'The Rich, I love them!', eh Simon?".
To give him credit, he didn't yell,
just raised his eyebrows like Harvey Keitel.
Yorkshire's finest Ayup Tarantino
mouthed Oh No No No No No No No No.
I fired 'in the style of' Jack Ruby -

get close to your man and let him have it.
The Big BANG BANG BANG. And all this for art.
Stitch that, I recall thinking. Where could I
shoot a poet, except through the heart?
Yeah, poetry should be as exciting
as going to movies. That quote I'd been
wanting to use for years, and at last seen
the point of. *Reservoir Dogs. Pulp Fiction.*
His last words, I wrote them down readily:
"Come in, Doctor fucking Polidori!"
[Screams. Fainting by Sponsors. Hand-held camera]

Holy-Roll- You-Over-In- The-Clover!
And his nostrils were dilated metaphors.
And his hands were cascading pages.
And his face was a picture withdrawn from auction.
And his ribcage was a canvas by Bacon.
And his jacket was a contract to present 'Cancelled'.
And his feet were the famous flat vowels.
And his legs were Saatchi posters, i.e. not working.
And his blood and guts were a load of tripe.
And his velvet moleskin sneakers were really quite stylish.

Hot-foot from the case of poor Jan Dildo,
a copper came; an arresting so-and-so.
DCI 'Nipper' Condom of the Yard,
(likes the odd backhander, and loves The Bard).
"Well, the fact of the matter is - you're nicked.
This whatsisname poet hath the bucket kicked.

136

And you're standing around in a string vest,
suspiciously like Cary Grant in *North By North West*".
Posed for pictures, I swore to tell the truth.
I'm thanked for not putting a bullet through the roof.

Tears which have threatened in previous scenes
will hold off no longer. I have lost, we
have all lost, a dear friend - one full of beans.
Let's strike a match in his dear memory
and think of his flickering flame. Snuffed it.
All that Millennium Buggery! He thought it
would last forever. His timing was wrong.
At Buckingham Palace, a New Year Gong
would lie uncollected. And SKY TV
must give up plans for prime time poetry.

The police advised me not to make amends
by going to the funeral. The aftermath,
tabloid and broadsheet mourning. Not since Plath,
not since Thomas, had death seemed poetic.
The pillars on which national life depends
were shaken for days. Paxman himself, sick
as he discussed How Can This Happen Here?
Who Now Can Be Old Ted's Stand-In On Earth?
Muldoon and Motion and an empty chair.
Melvyn Bragg and Peter Porter. Much mirth.

So that's me. Not Guilty! Like another
celebrity case that I could mention,
I'm being tried in Courts of Opinion,
with headline lawyers and fees, the Mother
of all Media scrums. A God-send
to my career, a typical 90s end.
To Judge Chutney, I've been coached to say
"It wasn't me. It's not true. See my play
on Channel 4, which reconstructs all fact"
(as if lying was simply Modern Tact).

They're trying to put me behind bars.
Yet I'm sponsored by Typhoo, Kodak and Mars.
Since being on remand, I'm in demand
by editors, columnists, porn stars. And
by Simon's spirit; I sense him at night.
In jail it's the Smell of the Cabbage alright.
And day by day, the wigged Judicial Muse
reconciles crossed words and contrary views:
"QCs, Mrs Blair! This is so...a crime,
proceedings must be conducted in rhyme.

Every hope must have its disappointment.
Every carefree fly finds its ointment.
For each stammerer there's a great talker,
each celebrity has their own stalker..."
Well, someone's got to be a right bastard.
He was Late Great enough to cut the mustard.
Zoom! was a pumping buttock of a book.
Kid its younger, softer brother.
Xanadu was great for the cabbage. Yuck.
Book of Matches? Struck out. Tuffluck, mother.

There are Natural Born Killers
and there is 'The Smell of the Cabbage'.
There's that daft show of Cilla's
and the smell of the cabbage.
Behind the Poetry Society bar
wafts the smell of the cabbage.
Not the young verse superstar -
just the smell of the cabbage
When I smell, I smell the smell of the cabbage.
And I think of him. I think of Simon Armitage.

I think of Simon Armitage.

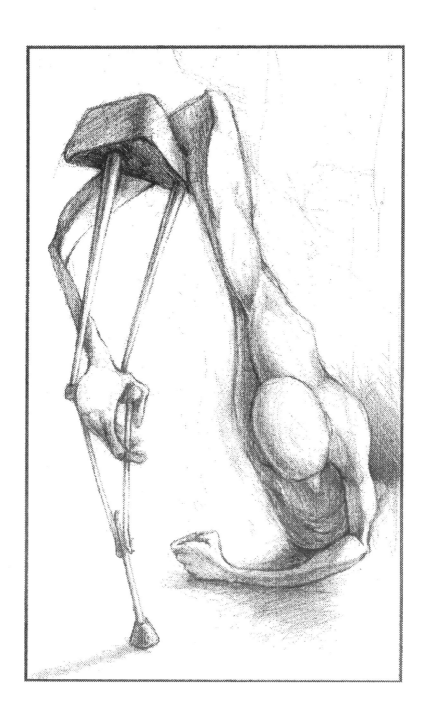

rodney wood
Farnborough, England

History

He came from a union in America,
birth attended by a locksmith and accountant.
Oxygen starvation. Lawyers called. There were oaths.
Commercial transactions. Silver rings welded to ears.

He was angry all the time, carved
on his neck was the number of
the beast but he had money, agony,
no purpose save one and that's me.

The people who remember him, his image
said he spoke like a hammer drill
from wheezing lungs; called everyone a bastard.
Had a contract out on his family.

Was a lunatic, wore green. The Devil hung
from his belt like a bunch of keys.

His eyes a bubble of aluminum and
glass, chewed a cigar as he asked
for cold filtered beer like it was
some ancient ceremony beside the beer stools.

The engine room in his gut pumped
non-stop, more fearsome than a cruise missile,
a nuclear powered submarine or a first
year medical student dissecting a black cat.

He wore an intercom on his ear,
wasn't afraid of the devil, winter landscapes
liked the poems of Hardy and Houseman,
belly like an oak barrel or Monet's Waterlilies.

Past 50, spent his time on the bog;
kept saying there's a bastard on his back.

Looking Straight Ahead - Robert Mitchum

I never passed the physical. Can't eat
much but it hasn't stopped me going
to restaurants, fancy dress parties and stripping,
covering myself with ketchup, standing on tables
and shouting *I'm a hamburger*. I'm getting
old, world-weary, wobbling with a girl on
each arm and holding my gut in.
I look like a wardrobe on castors.
Tough guy, joined a chain-gang as 91234.
Yet I wanted to write poetry, always
wanted to be a writer. But now
I get more money for less effort.
Acting's simple. It's just looking at the camera.
Scorsese said I was *noir*. I'm not impressed.

fred voss
Long Beach, USA

They Know How To Protect Their Own

The supervisor
wears such perfectly pressed spotlessly white shirts
and perfectly pressed pants and shined shoes
and glowing smiles
and walks with such a smooth authoritative walk
swinging his clipboard
and jotting down numbers with his pen
so masterfully
and appraising all situations and problems
with such confident knowingness
that by the time the machinists are about to see through
all of this
and realize that the supervisor is a completely incompetent
detriment to good machining and morale
and the company,
management
has already moved him
to another department on another shift
in another building.

High Wires And Ticking Clocks

The great ship coming into harbor sounds its horn
at 4 am
and water in glasses on tables beside the beds
of mothers going slowly insane
is still and smooth as glass
and all the rails of train tracks wait to ring
with wheels
and the high wire walker
stops to pick his teeth while looking at the moon
and old clocks tick in darkness
as cons
in cement cells try to make it one month more
and a man
cannot sleep for 3 nights because he wants to do
what is right
and 61-year-old men
working 60 hours a week try not to go insane
on assembly lines
and Judges' gavels
wait to be banged
and a million people
don't know what to do next
and the great ship's horn sounds again
out of the sea so vast it makes each of us
smaller than an atom
and somewhere someday someone will lift a pen and write a poem
people will never
stop wondering at
as the high wire walker makes it to the balcony of a building
or falls
into a page of history.

Birth At The Mouth Of A Blast Furnace

The slamming
of tons and tons of presses and drop hammers
down into the concrete floor of the steel mill all around my feet
over and over and over and over and over
all day
without end
was what I needed as it pounded my 23-year-old skin
and heart and mind until
it matched the slamming
inside me of the fear to put what I was
down on paper.
The searing
burning flame of the blast furnace
sucking the air out of my lungs
and stinging my lips and nostrils until they were as raw
as if they had been whipped
were what I needed
as it matched
the burning inside me of the shame
of the pen sitting unused on the dusty table
in the corner of my room,
and the steelworker men
with their hateful staring eyes and their stone jaws
and their closed fists
circling end circling me
were exactly what I needed as they crushed me
until i cracked
and finally poured all that slamming
and pounding and burning
and stinging and staring
out
across a page.

All The Perfectly Tied Shoelaces

Madness
in earth levelled
in 500 channels of tv
in endless surgery on the face to keep it young
Madness
in all the wound up watches
and filthy rivers madness
in the perfect order of pictures on a supervisor's desk
as he rides and threatens the employee
until he comes back in with the gun
Madness without one hair out of place
with an army or a country or a vast company
under it
with all the laws of the land behind it
Madness of all night electric bulbs
and factory production lines
Madness as American as apple pie
Madness that wins all the awards and climbs to the top
Madness of all the screaming of all the trees
chopped down
Madness in all the control panel buttons
and all the gas
pouring into all the gas tanks madness
in the spoiled rivers
in the coins stacked on the dresser
in the belt
and the smile pulled tight madness
that has never truly heard a foghorn
or seen a cloud move
or stopped for one brief second
to feel the rain.

And We Didn't Have To Die To Get There

In the height of summer the steel mill could get so hot
thermometers broke,
so hot
as waves of heat radiated up off the endless black
asphalt
all around the steel mill
and not one trace of air
moved in or out of all the big tin doors that had been rolled all the way open
all night
and big high velocity fans
did nothing but blow hot air in our faces
and the sun beat down on the tin roof
that we could barely move
in our steel-toed boots and face shields
as ice water
we had soaked paper towels in dripped
down the back of our necks
and the handles to our machines felt like branding irons,
so hot
that the time clock holding us between those tin walls
had never seemed so slow
or so cruel
or so insane
as it told us there was still work to do
and deadlines to meet
as we forced our arms and our legs to drag through their motions
and tried to breathe
as the white-hot flames licked the brick mouths of the blast furnaces
near us
and we knew
that Hell
could only have been invented
by men.

Dissertation On A Drop Of Sweat

I would rather
study the broken english of a Vietnamese engine lathe operator cursing
a hot steel chip
that has just sliced open his finger
or the sparkle and the spirit and the torment and the anger
in the eye of a man
whose fingers have grown gnarled and twisted
around the handles of a machine he has run
all his life barely keeping himself and his family alive
or the stub
of a woman's finger cut off on a graveyard shift sweatshop punch press
or a foreman
gone insane on a concrete floor with a clipboard in his hand
or the way
a man can still laugh like he has the world in the palm of his hand
as he walks out a factory door at the end of a day
after all that 30 years of 2-ton drop hammers
and 6,000-ton presses
slamming and pounding and screaming
have done to him
or the dirt under his fingernails
or the lines
carving his face
or the cuff of his pants waving in the air
as he walks
or the grease-and-oil-smeared sweaty T-shirt
twisted across his back
or the sunlight on his shoulder or on the brim of his beat-up
fisherman's hat
or a trickle of foam falling from the lip of a schooner of beer
into his beard
or any word
so real and rough and unschooled
out of his mouth and his great heart
that no book could ever begin to capture

154

than Shakespeare or Shelley
or any word. of any Ph.D. dissertation
I might ever have written.

Trying To Keep Our Feet On Planet Earth

"Making any spaceship parts?"
a machinist will ask another machinist
as he passes him at his machine
carving aluminum
into aircraft parts.
"Made any parts for your spaceship lately?"
machinists
will ask each other when washing up at the end of a day's work
and laugh
heartily like nothing could be more absurd
though
somewhere in a dark corner of their psyches
there may be a grain of doubt
when they remember Clarence
over on machine #559
who really did end up making parts for his spaceship
whenever he could squeeze them in between jobs
before he landed in the State Mental Hospital
and Houston
over on the turret lathe who came to believe
aliens hovering in invisible craft over our machine shop
were pummeling his brain with gamma rays
and consider
how easy it is for men who work at Goodstone Aircraft Company all their lives
to end up
in outer space.

156

Drop Hammers And Dilated Eyes

The Verson 6,000-ton metal-bending press
roared
and slammed until our hearts trembled as Wallace
prowled the building staring at electrical control boxes and panels
and looking for hidden cameras
because every night since the aliens had abducted him
and planted a computer chip in his brain
he had stayed awake thinking of ways to escape them
as they spied on him and tried to control him.
The blast furnaces
roared with white-hot flame as they sucked
the oxygen out of our lungs and sent the stink
of our burning beards up our nostrils
as Vietnam vets
sat motionless at machines for hours sweating
with dilated eyes like they were a hair's-breadth away from cracking
and exploding
into mayhem
and Chicago who had spent 7 years in the pen
and fried his brain on speed
sat at an automatic drill press
slapping a 3-foot-long section of lead pipe into his palm
over and over one thousand times a day
to let us know that he would fight
at the drop of a hat
and the 2-ton drop hammers sent shock waves through our hearts
and shook our nerves and the concrete floor under our feet
and hundreds of sparkling blue flashes of welding rods
blinded us
and planted headaches deep in our brains and we wondered
which was the greater cross to bear,
all of these great machines stinking
and screaming and burning and cutting and pounding their way through us,
or ourselves.

Gods That Tick And Blast And Beep

We have worked away our lives
to the time clocks,
metal boxes
that stamp red letters along the edges of cards we stick into them
or plastic computerized boxes with slots
we run magnetized strips on our photo id badges through,
racing in our cars
through traffic and hurrying in our steel-toed shoes across concrete
toward them
and standing before them
in lines at the end of days and weeks with heads bowed
waiting for that final tick of a minute
when all our chains fall away from us.
Buzzers
or whistles loud enough to make our skin crawl
and our hearts jump
blast out of bull horns mounted high up on tin walls
all our lives
as alarm clocks stab and shake us awake in pitch dark mornings
and we stare
at clocks on tin walls from behind our factory machines,
clocks
that hold our spirits in each tick
of their second hands,
clocks
that we have looked at more than the words
in all our Bibles or the eyes
of our wives
and children,
clocks
that tick away all that we might have been
as they crawl
toward all that we cannot escape.

Fan Shortage

I was new to the building and the fan
was behind Howard's machine.
It was pointed away from his machine
up at a far away corner of the tin ceiling
50 feet above
and so far through all the increasingly-hot summer
I had never seen it turned on,
so
one day when I hadn't seen Howard anywhere near his machine
for over an hour
and the pushing-100 degree heat was making the sweat drip
off my nose and the back of my neck
as I nodded on the edge of sleep in my chair
I walked over and grabbed the 6-foot-tall high-velocity
fan and carried it over to my machine
and turned it on
and sat fully awake and alert and cooled and happy
until Howard
appeared out of nowhere with his hands indignantly planted
on his hips and a furious expression on his face.
"HEY! That's my FAN!"
he screamed, unplugging the fan and wrapping his arms around it.
"YOU'RE GONNA HAVE TO PAY FOR THIS! YOU CAN'T BE TAKING MY
GODDAMNED FUCKING FAN AWAY!"

Then he carried the fan back to behind his machine where he left it unplugged
and pointed away at the far corner of the ceiling again
for the rest of the day.

richard whelan

London, England

Community Service Blues

Through security grates
clotheslines strung across balconies
of a notorious estate

A wind manufactured by express trains
breezing a cold sweat
from the hems of long skirts, babyclothes,
grey overalls ....

Each day you paint rockinghorses blue
Build a tower of them under a railway arch
like Franz Marc

Working off a debt to society for Santa Claus
while Big Steve daubs an elephant lime green
and inbetween... Middle aged Jamaican ladies
converse frankly on sexual mores
with young English white boys
as they make the workshop tools whine and sing

Big Steve, a chauffeur, says he chinned a copper
who cut him up and scratched his motor
Now has 200 hrs to kill
in his elephants graveyard of wooden puzzles
"Could've been worse" he laughs
Xmas inside
Yellow walls
and a pot to piss in

Another long teabreak, you cram your mouth
with tunafish breadrolls, coffee and cigarettes
Go outside watch the rain fall
on a dead allotment
Tomorrow a muddy puddle
            a muddled puzzle
                Big Steve is just beginning to solve.

Pain Threshold

New blemishes and abrasions
The plum coloured polka dots
made by knucklebones
Or anointing a graze
with a swab of violet iodine
Our bodies bruise
in such fervid chameleon hues
Yellow and blue roses
concussing the epidermis
Bringing the exhilaration
of fairground carousels
wheeling our flesh
to an exultant flush
as the world tilts
and we go under
the hooves
of a dancing
screaming
horse.

Stock Answer

If you want to know
why the white veil dropped by a bird
adorns your forehead
and not the forehead
of another passing in the crowd
Ask around
Petition God
or a passing windowcleaner
Your best friend from childhood
or the mad monk who mixes your medicine
Ask those calling sweetly in the trees
and you'll get the same stock answer
The same bird whistling
how nobody knows nobody cares.

greta stoddart
London, England

Switzerland

What an elaborate co-production
(Italo-Franco-German), I thought,
for really such a simple tale
involving three plumbers, granted
all of different shape and size,
and a towering buxom blonde in a slip.

There was nothing else to do.
The flat was luxury, done out in white
from top to bottom except the wall
-to-wall 3-inch pile which was cream.
You could see Lake Geneva,
calm as a mirror outside the window.

Dressed in overalls and big boots,
two of them have stockings over their heads
but the little one's in charge so it's him who gets
to peek through the spy-hole at her,
pink feather duster in hand, bending
over the sofa, her frilly arse.

I get up as late as possible.
There's milky coffee and a *Herald Tribune*
gets delivered. There's a long shower
and me wrapped up in soft, white towels.
There's a lover somewhere across two borders
up to his knees in a dirty war.

The doorbell rings and she turns round.
Then she's up against the fridge,
her big lipstick mouth - *nein... nein...*
The stocking heads hold her down
and there's a close-up of the little one's face,
a sound of ripping above the music.

There are children hanging from the trees;
he writes he won't be home for Christmas.
I lie back on the King-size bed.
The mountains are dark on the other side.
The towel drops open, sunlight pours in;
I spit on my fingers, press rewind.

Pegasus

On the edge of town where the road
rises like a ramp into the sky,
a pony stands in the middle of a field,
hoof-deep in mud as if entranced
by something beyond the constant cars.

Nobody has ever seen that pony
out of the field nor the field
without the pony. Nobody has ever
seen it ridden or fed or led
in or out of the field. Some say
they had to build the road around it.

Not that we cared. We weren't interested
in things we could see, turning inward
as children do as soon as they know
the first stories, bending their heads
to tend to secrets, to preparation.

Taking the shoebox into the wood,
we'd spread our drawing out on the ground:
a horse ascending feint lines,
astride him two girls clutching his mane,
and in the bubble above their heads,
Please come and take us away!

And after one long embrace
we'd open our eyes, certain to see it,
massive and white and stamping,
its mad, steaming head, its wings
erect and twitching in the light.

I don't remember disappointment;
just an empty clearing, the slight
rattle of leaves, the distant cars.

The No 4

"You'll wait forever for the No 4!" our driver shouts
to someone out in the rain and slides the doors with a hiss.
The bus turns quiet and pulls away, swaying like a cradle.
No one smiles but we're quite content because we're moving
and outside the night is black and freezing but we're inside
smelling of rain and iron and sugary breath.

Turning the corner we see, huddled together under
the shelter, a group of little bodies inside winter coats.
They stand alone, their sullen legs stuffed into boots.
Their heads are bowed and their hair is neatly oiled
and parted down the middle so we can see the chalky
path of every scalp, the sliver of bone in every neck.

Lifting their heads in unison, it's as if they know
already they won't believe what they are about to see.
A tired kind of innocence has turned their eyes to water
and tbeir skin is white and smooth as wax and each one
has a long and wiry beard that drags along the ground,
dipping its wispy ends into the puddles of rain.

One lifts an arm to hail the bus but his limbs are heavier
than the weight of bone and his hand trembles as he holds out
a faded blue ticket. He peers up through tbe driving dark.
His face is young and shines like a silent movie star,
brimming with a hopeless kind of beauty. And his beard,
his beard keeps blowing in the wind like some terrible joke.

But our driver won't stop. Our driver drives on, shaking his bead.
And inside the bus is as quiet as ever, the night as black.
We turn and see the children have hung their heads once more.
Their beards glow like will-o'-the wisp in the dark.
The streetlamp watches over them like a nurse or guardian angel,
head inclined but with no wings to gather them in.

172

To Day

Poor Day. Poor undaunted, faithful Day.
You bore me. All you make me want to do
is sleep through your long, colourless stay
and conscientiously object to

the march of time you keep so well. Poor Day,
save the light you have onIy God and the birds
(who no one sees) who fly like hymnbooks, frail,
hysterical, in the drab arch of your world.

You've had your day, Day. Or so it seems.
And I'm sliding, like a hand into a dark glove,
to where there is light you couldn't even dream of,
where we infidels find beauty, are beloved.

O Day, forgive me, won't you, this turning away.
These dark eyes I own grow darker by the day.

maurice rutherford

Bridlington, England

His Letter She'd Kept

Thanks, Mum, for yours of – when, three months ago? Or more?
Spain was *simpática* in Spring; and Portugal.
Ta, also, for the birthday card – at Estremoz –
yes, fortyfive feels much the same as fortyfour!
But Summer came too hot, my hands broke out again
and so the hitch back north through France and Germany.

One lift, from Hamburg, took me up to Gothenburg-
Volvo Estate, ex-hippie Swede – phenomenal!
Wow, Gothenburg was way out, man; live, green and neat,
though prices were four times as high as those in Spain
or double what you'd have to pay in Hull or Brid.
I found some borage seed oil – healed my hands a treat.

So, Finland now. I'm lodging in this wooden house
and need to have the windows well blacked-out at night
for sleep, the sky's so bright – or otherwise I lie
awake and in the nightglow sometimes find myself
almost remembering those rhymes we learnt from you
as kids. Send me the words again, next time you write?

Here, Summer weather's late, much rain; wild strawberries
abound, and blueberries. I mainly live off fish
caught overnight. The water's only slightly salt,
and shallows round the coastline teem with perch and pike
some flounders, too – remember Donna Nook? Best dish
I've had were smoked above an alder sawdust fire.

Sometimes, across the fields, I've seen a cautious elk.
I doubt I'll ever catalogue the many birds.
From Turku Abo recently I watched the start
of what the locals told me was the Tall Ships' Race
and spotted one whose port of registry was Hull!
Dawn now, and time to check my nets. Tell me the words.

Waterloo Bridge

Strange accent, "...twenty pence...a cup of tea...
an interview tomorrow for a job...".
I hesitate, afraid I might get mugged,
then cough up 50p and wish him well,
rejoin the others crossing Waterloo
and wonder why it was he singled me;

is it so obvious I'm on a high,
first London night I've had in umpteen years,
big evening at the South Bank, fee to come,
accommodation paid-for, train-fare home?
Could easily have given him five quid,
or nothing, clenched my shoulders, barged on by,

but chose the easy cop-out coin instead -
a somehow gesture to a somewhere son
of twice his age and living lord knows how -
walked on by Aldwych (Chekhov, Judi Dench)
then up Southampton Road to Woburn Place,
my rancid B & B, a fusty bed.

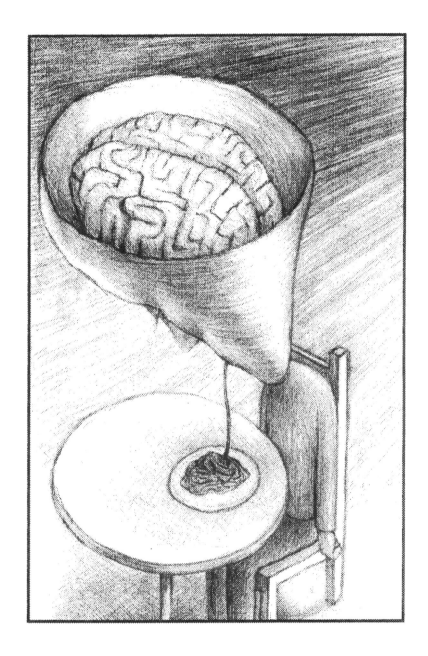

james prue
Sussex, England

No.17 Retford Place

When the police came round,
John woke me up.
He seemed to have grown up over night.

I got up from my bed on the floor,
the police asked me some questions,
then left.

John told us his willy
had been hanging out of his boxers
when he opened the door to them.

But no one laughed,
because Stuart was dead
and it was as if it was
all our fault.

Not Quite Grown up No.1

Struggling to carry
my toast in one hand
and the job description
in the other
I fumble and trip
smearing marmite
on my blue T-shirt
and scattering paper
across the floor

It is a childish mess
I am not surprised though
because, though I am twenty four,
I don't seem to have
quite grown up yet.

Bastards

Having returned home
to be reunited with television
and parents

It seems like
the most viciously hurtful
bad joke
that the pictures on screen
are trying to entice me
to buy a B.M.W

ben myers
London, England

The Greek Girl's Arse

She had the most fantastic arse imaginable.

I wish that I was American so that I could say ass, but I'm not. I'm European, I'm British. I say arse. I say it long and drawn out with the definition on the 'r'. arrrrrrrrs.

She was Greek, she worked in the family restaurant and she had the most fantastic arse imaginable. I was there with my girlfriend, drinking watered-down house white wine and waiting for something to eat. The food wasn't fantastic, but she was. Her arse was full and protruding like a ripe watermelon squeezed into a short black skirt, but it wasn't big and it wasn't fat. It was perfect, almost in a detached way as if it was added to her body as an afterthought or as if it had grown from a seed that landed on her flat buttocks eighteen months ago. This wasn't sexual, it was much bigger. This was art, this was religion, this was more perfect than anything man or machine could deliberately create. This was a biological result of pure magnificence.

I had to tell my girlfriend.

"Have you seen the waitress's arse?"

"Which one?" She politely asked, without squirming around in her seat to stare at the ladies passing with wine carafes, saucers of olives, peppers and so forth.

"She's behind you. Long dark hair, brown eyes, rump. Wait a minute. You'll see who I mean immediately. I can't believe it, it's too wonderful. I can't believe it, it can't be real."

Sure enough a minute later she walked past us to the bar to fill another tray with drinks. All I could see was the arse straining to burst out of her skirt. I was hypnotised.

"Christ," murmured my girlfriend, licking her lips and sipping some iced water. "You're right. It's a peach, a big old juicy peach...hmmmm"

We tried to be subtle but our eyes followed her around the room.

We couldn't help it. We were captivated.

"She shouldn't be kept a secret here in this badly-lit restaurant."

"I know. She should be held aloft and paraded through the streets." We ate some peppers in silence, glancing up from time to time for progress reports. What made this unknown girl's arse so hypnotic was that I knew that it wasn't flawless and it wouldn't last.

"It's not going to last." I whispered through a mouthful of bread. "Can't you see it?"

"What do you mean?"

"I mean, it's so perfect because it's now and we both know that it will never last. Picture her in ten, twenty, thirty years' time. How many old Greek women do you see with – "

"Such a juicy posterior? You're right. It's juicy but it's going to fall. All fruit rots and dies."

"You can almost see it within. I mean, you can almost see the future pushing down on her because that arse is young. Within in it something but bigger and paler and uglier and maybe covered in blue veins or pimples struggling to get out."

"How can nature create something so beautiful and then distort it or corrupt it."

"It's gravity. It hits us all. One day she'll be fat and that arse will be hanging over the edge of a toilet seat. She'll have had a handful of kids, eaten the wrong things, not retained her figure, it's an impossibility for an arse like that to remain unchanged."

"But it's so...perfect."

We sipped our drinks in silence. I tried an olive. She chewed on a slice of carrot. The waitress with the greatest arse in the world carried on filling orders. Neither of us spoke, we were deep in our thoughts of death and decay. The perfect arse had made us think too hard. The perfect arse had tainted the night. We drank onwards, smoking cigarettes from time to time.

Arrrrrrrs.

Bobby And The Seven Dogs' Tails

Bobby had seven dogs' tails in his bottom drawer. The two drawers above contained the usual type of things: underpants, socks, shirts. Various girlfriends had bought most of the underwear and clothing for him over the past few years. The tails, however he had cut off himself. Acquiring dogs was easy; it was the actual cutting that was the hardest part. Tails can be pretty tough sometimes.

All of the dogs had come from around his area. If you took a map and drew a line from Kennington to Camberwell to Brixton and then back to Kennington you'd have a Bermuda Triangle for dogs. No one realised that dogs were going missing, though, apart from their owners. If someone was doing their job probably they'd notice that there were seven dogs trotting around South London without tails. If all the owners had all been friends, then Bobby might have had a problem on his hands. But they didn't, so his little kidnappings went unnoticed.

Bobby wasn't cruel, he never killed any of the dogs. He just cut off their tails like other people snip the stalks of daffodils. He had seven tails and they were all from different breeds. After he cut the tail off and the dog had stopped howling Bobby carefully sterilised the stump and bandaged it up nicely. He had steady hands and a gentle bedside manner. Bobby wasn't insane either, the only strange thing he did was cut seven tails off seven dogs. Keeping them was a little bizarre too, but after he'd gone to the trouble of procuring the dogs it seemed a waste to throw them away.

Bobby liked to take them out of the drawer and lay them out on his bed to look at them. They were all different colours and different lengths. Sometimes he just forgot about them and went about getting on with his life.

If Bobby invited you into his flat you wouldn't know that there were seven dogs tails in his bottom drawer. Things are like that sometimes. Maybe your wife or uncle has animal parts in their bedroom. Maybe they've had sexy dreams about cartoon characters. Maybe they've they sent postcards to themselves.

Bobby started playing golf recently. He's got his handicap down to eighteen.

Literary Rejections Are What Make A Man

Dear Ben
Thank you for sending us your play for
consideration
Unfortunately
(don't say it)
after careful
(don't say it)
consideration
our panel of
(nazis)
readers has decided that
your play
(don't say it motherfucker)
will not be taken any further.
(damn, you said it)
The dialogue is
snappy
(yes)
and has a certain
bite
to it
(I'll bite your ass, fool)
but you have to decide
what it is about
(like everything: nothing)
and what it is you want
to comment on.
We would like to thank you
(no, thank you)
for entering your play
and to
encourage you
to
(give up?)
keep up with your writing.
We wish you
(death, pestilence)
good luck in your future
(suicide)
writing.
Yours sincerely, the end.

192

The Contract

The contract stipulates
that
your balls belong to them.
From now on
your sleep
your stubble
your liver trouble
belongs to them.
The contract stipulates
that
your time is not
your own
9 a.m.
and you want
to slip it in
as she sleeps
but you can't:
your balls belong to them.
College education
leaking toilet cistern
empty bottle, still
your balls belong to them.
The dust
the dreams
the music
belong to you
but
your balls belong to them

simon armitage
Huddersfield, England

The Flags of the Nations

THE LAW REQUIRES THAT IT IS ESSENTIAL TO USE THE CORRECT COLOURED BAG AT ALL TIMES.

White Nylon with Orange Band;	ALL PATIENTS' PERSONAL SOILED (dirty) CLOTHING.
White Nylon;	ALL SOILED (dirty) laundry and net bags.
Clear Plastic;	Laundry FOULED with faecal matter, blood, bile, vomit or pus. Fouled items should be placed into a clear plastic bag, and then into a white nylon outer bag.
Clear Water-Soluble;	INFESTED (body lice and fleas)
Red Water-Soluble;	INFECTED laundry, if soiled, from patients with or suspected of suffering from Hepatitis A or B, Typhoid, Paratyphoid, Salmonella, Shigella, Cholera, Anthrax, Poliomyelitis, Diphtheria & HIV.
	All such infested/infected laundry should be placed into the appropriate water-soluble bag and then sealed in an outer bag.
Green Plastic;	THEATRE linen only.
Yellow Plastic;	Clinical waste for incineration.
Black Plastic;	Non-infected household-type waste only. Papers. Flowers.

david hernandez
Cerritos, USA

Death Wish

Moments after you toss a coin
down the dark tunnel
of a well, a twig snaps
behind your back.

You turn around
and the Grim Reaper
waves to you,
his bony fingers clattering

like dull wind chimes.
Slowly he raises his scythe
over his hooded skull.
The curved blade flashes

in the moonlight,
sighs as it slices
the air you have always
filled your lungs with

until now.

charles bennet
Lancashire, England

William Wordsworth's Socks

As if a single drop of rain
from all the deep protracted rush

which smashed the mere
to a miserable blur

had been preserved – I found,
nestled at the end of memory

like a pair of inverted commas
closing a lively correspondence

of which nothing else remained,
your old grey socks;

quiet and tidy and labelled
with a set of neat initials

they waited patiently as dogs:
watching the rain with one eye open

wanting to go for a walk.

b. a. j. evans
Cambridge, England

Almost

she had long hair
that fell
down

to
her tits

and her eyes were dark

and he could hear her
whisper

"come and get
it!"

he hooted and began to
work himself

up
in front of her.

she remained
unflinched,

quietly staring from the couch
with her

legs apart.

he could almost smell the
girlie part of

her from where he stood
and then

something frustrating dropped
in

as he worked himself into a
frenzy

and in the end his left hand
gave it up

he
threw

the mag
back into the top drawer

a. a. dodd
London, England

White Christmas And Cold Turkey

The streets are filled with cocaine
three foot deep.

I can barely sleep at all tonight
I can barely sleep at all.

Don't know whether to snore or snort
take a nap or do a line
plenty of lemon
(barley)
forget the lime.

Snow
three foot deep
gobbled by snowmen with carrots for noses
and buttons like saucers for eyes.

Prize fighter columbians
white shadows in straight thin lines
divvying out what's yours and mine on sledges
the edges built upon razor blades.

Shades of Al Pacino
Gian Luca Vialli
snow three foot deep
I can barely sleep at all tonight
I can barely sleep at all.

dave wright
Bridlington, England

Eldorado

Arcade networks of cabled foreheads
allow only the weight of malice through,
the bulk of bottled ire
restrained beneath the veneer.

In a fruit machine,
mirrored on the tally-line,
eyes of a beaten contender.

In tune to the rhythm
of the electronic cacophony
the knuckle outline of stressful tendency
releases the arm in violent recoil.

Cylinders come to rest
-one at lemon, one at lime,
the third at cherry.

The resonation of a further coin
reverberates
in the violated slot.

gordon mason
Brighton, England

A Laying-On Of Hands

Hard to sit and watch you fade
like this. But the lightness your
illness brings makes you sometimes
spry of mind - these are the *up-days*

when I might expect to find you
peering at the luminescence of
a grandchild's skin, or telling it
of making jam, or baking bread,

just as you might have done
had you been the one for
making jam, or baking bread,
all those years ago.

Sometimes, you spend a whole day
searching for that piece of paper –
the one you're sure you'll need
if ever you're required to show it.

Other times you spend the day
just touching things,
moving slowly round the house
picking up and putting down -

meaning to enjoy the memory
each holds but somehow looking
through them, past them.
So more and more now, as I

watch you settle in your chair,
your gently folded hands remind me
of some frail-winged butterfly the next
cool, Autumn day might take.

ian parks
Mexborough, England

Promises and Smiles

We live under a government
of promises and smiles.

Out here you wouldn't know it:
the pit-heads are grassed over,

ice cracks the frozen lake
and under last night's sealing frost

the hills are white for miles.
The city where I leave you

bears the weight: it groans
under a winter sky

these bright new stars transfix
where every hoarding shows a face

and each converted loft contains
a hive of millionaires.

Is this where the heart
and commerce meet -

in a loose affiliation
of our little love affairs

with what is gained and what is lost?
Redress these beggars

in the mindless street,
the rule of love and politics.

andrew parker
Liverpool, England

Straightener

I met the fucker
by the caves
in Sefton Park,
the straightener
was on.

His boys sat back
in a silver Merc,
I'd come alone; mistake?

He came on strong
but amateurish.
Hit me 'round a bit,
I gauged his weight
then I knew
he was easy.

I twatted him a good one
in the ribs. CRUNCH!
He crumpled like a
burnt match.
While he wailed
I inflicted some damage.
Head, knees, ankles.

I looked at the Merc,
his boys stayed put.
Aah, delinquent probity.

I walked away, smiling.
I'd won.

She's mine now.

michael curran

Surrey, England

Who Needs Rain In The Afternoon?

I came straight
away.

And she swallowed it.

I fell in love with
her at that moment.

I refused to kiss
her until she had
brushed her teeth.

Love conquers most
things, but not basic
hygiene.

dean wilson
Hull, England

Get Your Cock Out My Arse I Can Feel A Poem Coming On

He led me up the garden path
and beyond
He was built like a brick shit house
and women fond

We met in a lay-by
on the way to Brid
he offered me a tenner
to suck his dick

I said "I don't do it for money
I do it for love
but if you insist
thankyou very much"

I sucked him until
he was high as a kite
I sucked him to within
an inch of his life

I sucked him until
he begged for mercy
I sucked him until
he came over my jersey

It took him a while
to come down
but when he did
his gratitude knew no bounds

He offered to take me
for a ride in the country
I said "I've got a better idea
put it away and come with me"

So I took him home
and did him his tea
Nowt special
just a Linda McCartney

He filled his face
and said "That was smashing"
My heart fluttered
like summat out of Jane Austen

It dint take him long
to get undressed
He stood there in all his glory
I was more than impressed

He was smaller than some
bigger than most
Before I knew where I was
I was touching my toes

His hands were everywhere
I felt a bit queasy
I said "I'm all for self expression
but is this absolutely necessary?"

He said "aye, it is
just relax
a few more inches to go
you'll soon get the knack"

I said "I don't think I will
I'm feeling a bit faint
and by the looks of it my skirting boards
could do with a lick of paint"

daithidh macEochaidh
York, England

Taidhg Ruadh Takes Off his Trilby

Sick and tired of poetry
as interesting woolly cardigans
with leather patches at the elbow,
written by middle class hicks
who know all the correct mosses
and lichens to produce a really
authentic Harris Tweed Jacket
that can babble and cant about
the dialectics of dialect or
symbolic grammar; give me the
one-liner to knee-cap the vicar
with some sonnet to bugger
the Queen Mother's corgies,
the sort of rhyme as slick
as kecking your own verses
after fifteen pints and a vindaloo,
tell me a couple of lines that'll
make me girlfriend cum quicker,
how about a chant to fill stands,
how about a rant that gets the bailiffs
breakdancing bragging about how
they are in touch with their female side,
how about a witty aside that makes
the bankmanager hand out the spliffs
and masturbate quite openly in front of you,
no more poems as English as a dead language,
no more carefully structured wallpaper
with dado rails for titles and fake stone
cladding of re-worked over-worked forms
on their second mortgage and third marriage,
and for all those woolly jumpers, Harris Tweed,
coffee table tosspots, the sort of scum that come
armed for a reading with Edwardian Dictionaries,
go eat my shit if all you can do is re-cycle
the bottle bank of broken stanzas stale
as yesterday's soiled duds

208

jon summers
Gwent, Wales

Alive, Alight

You live for
the rush
of your horse crossing
the finishing post,
first,
at sixteen-to-one.

Going to pick: up your winnings,
picking the next race.

Warm.
Full of adrenalin.
Alive,
and aware of it,
brilliantly,
now.

janet oliver
Broadstairs, England

Down the Pit

The coal mine next door
is like a secret cave
where eager diggers get sucked in.

Will you fall into the open pit
and explore the darkness there
with your lantern burning bright?

You could travel down its tunnels
hammering deeper, further away from me
because I swing in your cage
squawking, 'Give me oxygen,'
much too often.

Sometimes when I imagine
that I see soot in your hair
and black fingerprints on my feathers,
I yearn for the stuffiness of that cage
and pray you'll never wear your hard hat
down someone else's mine.

fiona curran
London. England

The Incomplete Inventory

Like you, I have libraries, all the usual,
books, music, magazines, people. Almost all aligned,
all made easy to find, the dusty corners
of brooding minds swept clean enough
for me to define their categories. Yet one or two
are still not fit for inventory, especially you, my love,
who I should confine, to light romance,
on reflection, maybe gothic.

At first I thought you sensitive,
imagined a large book of coloured plates,
highland fauna, shaded as delicately
as a restricted grasp of the palate would allow.
A nineteenth century botanist on the make
as humbly as he knew how, wide strides
pushing forth, a little more, man's knowledge.
I saw your wire rims washed with rainbow rain,
your body tilt into mountain terrain, searching.
A blushing picture.

After a year or so, I changed my tune
and you became the detailed case notes
of Freud or Jung, at least something of a mystery.
The twists and turns of your psyche's pride, led you
to cast plain love aside, in favour of the new.
So again roaming. "Abandon her", inside you cried
and as I was never the out door type, I don't blame you.
Still, you have been, more than many, a useful book
in your time; you even came cunningly disguised
as the best blank verse. But as, beloved,
we can't go on, who cares for last chapters ?

We both keep books that are unread, flipped through,
used as reference or skimmed for their meat. One day,
further down the line, with new acquisitions made,
we can donate each other to new shelves,
there to be filed by different hands, not yet knowing
where they'll put us, but, to have a guess, my darling,
I'd say large print melodrama.

denise duhamel

Miami, USA

No Home-Wrecker

When I was twenty, I kissed a man
much older than I was. My drunk hand found
a strange indent and lump of flesh
on the back of his waist, an extra little potbelly.
I quickly moved my fingers away and grabbed
onto his shoulder instead. After the kiss,
the man immediately told me he was married. For years
my memory had it that I slapped him and left the party,
a friend's cramped Beacon Hill apartment.
But now I think what happened
is that he began to cry, just slightly, so that at first
I thought his wet eyes had something to do with an allergy.
Then he said he really loved his wife and needed
air. We took baby steps, holding hands,
through the slippery cobblestone streets,
snow settling on my eyelashes, in his beard.
We slipped into a diner where our coats and scarves
dripped puddles onto the floor.
He told me a long story about married life--
her chemotherapy, how he'd just lost his job.
I sobered up and looked at my plate of pale scrambled eggs,
what I imagined cancer looked like,
what I imagined fat looked like under the skin.
I poked my fork around, curious
to see that spare tire, that love handle of his.
He kept blowing his nose, his cheeks fat and pink
like the soles of a newborn's feet.
The rest of him looked lean in his wooly sweater,
then he seemed to shrink even smaller
as he put back on his oversized overcoat to walk me home.
I felt rejected when he left me at my door
and disappeared into a flurry, thanking me for listening.
The story I told my friends who were at the party
was that OK, he was kind of cute, but I was
no home-wrecker. The story I told myself
was that I'd have never done anything like that--
his wife had cancer for god's sake.
Now that I look back, the man was probably only
in his late thirties, about the age I am now.
He had no money so I wound up covering our diner check,
emptying the last of my change on the table for too small a tip.

Snapshots From A Stolen Camera

Maybe the man who stole our camera on the Paris RER
will sell it to a Latin Quarter pawn shop owner who
will in turn sell it to a lovely woman on her baby's first birthday.
She'll go to load the camera with her own film and find
a roll already in there with ten or so pictures left.
It'll flash through her mind, "I wonder if this camera is stolen?"
Then her daughter, just new to walking, will tumble on the carpet,
nothing serious, and start to cry. The mother will remember
she still has to put up the decorations and begin to unwind
a roll of red crepe paper and twirl it around her small,
but charming living room while comforting her baby
with a French song. When the guests
arrive with the baby's bright gifts, the mother will reach for the camera.
She'll snap her daughter eating fistfuls of gooey cake
and finish the roll of film my husband and I began.
The next day she'll bring the Kodak to be developed
and the first snapshots she'll see will be of my husband, then me
on the giant Ferris wheel in the park across the street from
the Louvre. The Eiffel Tower will twinkle behind us
in early twilight. She'll see that we sat across from each other
in tea-cup like cars, passing the camera back and forth,
taking pictures on the way up, on the way down,
over the scary hump at the top.
The woman will stare at our faces and remember her ex,
her daughter's father, who didn't even have the decency
to show up at the party. She'll say, "Fuck you," to us
in French and contemplate ripping our pictures up
because we look so happy. But then she'll remember
the stubble on her old love's chin, the perfect
half-moon curve of his ear. She'll wonder if my husband
and I are rich or poor, if we come to Paris every year
or if this was the one great trip of our lives. She'll wonder
if we were hurt when the robber took our camera--
if we were held at knife-point or just
careless with our knapsack at a busy café.
Before she gets to the photos of her daughter's party,
she'll see my husband standing in front of the Hotel Notre Dame,

the last picture I took before we were robbed.
Just then, her baby will gurgle and she'll feel so lucky
to have her daughter and a wonderful camera
with a flash and a zoom, a lens cap and a handy strap.
She'll put the snapshots of my husband and me in a brown bag
and drop them off at the Hotel Notre Dame
next time she's in the neighborhood, her baby in the stroller
and a baguette under her arm. she'll write a note
that reads, "Will you please see that the people in these pictures
get them?" The clerk will remember us--
"Ah, those Americans." He'll look up our names
in the registrar and copy our New York address
onto a padded envelope and slip in the photographs
with the young mother's anonymous note. By the time the photographs
arrive, my husband and I will be back to our old routine.
We won't believe how good we looked--
the way my curls blew in the Ferris wheel breeze
as though a professional stylist were in the next car
with a fan and cans of hair spray.
I must have looked at least ten pounds thinner
as I went over the top, and my husband--
well, he looked as though he was starring
in a Tommy Hilfiger ad. Or maybe what happened is
that the thief pulled out our film,
then tossed it into a train station trash can
so that by nightfall it was covered with empty Evian bottles
and crumpled candy wrappers. Maybe,
though it was against his policy,
the thief kept our Minolta for himself
to take pictures of his own kid.
Or maybe he sold it to a friend to feed his family
or a drug habit that he's been trying to kick.
Maybe the woman bought a different, less fancy camera.
Maybe the baby's birthday wasn't for another month.
Maybe there was never any woman at all--
but those snapshots, I'm sure they would have turned out swell--
so sparkly, so glamorous, so very Paris.

david lyall
London, England

Cut and Dried

Years of staring at the backs of heads took its toll
and hairspray began to catch the back of the throat.
Day after day the heads came, the hair fell
over the shoulders onto the floor, and thoughts

of all that dry, dead stuff began to choke.
You dreamt of pillows full of tangled hair
and mattresses and duvets, and when you woke
there were scissors in your bed and shreds of cotton everywhere.

But the phone kept ringing, filling the book
with pages of perms and blow-dries and trims
and more people with photos who "wanted to look
like them." Daily reflections in the mirror grew more dim.

Then what you'd run your hands through betrayed
you like a lover, and that which you'd treated like a slave
rose up in uncontrollable tufts, curls laid
themselves flat, perms failed and finally something gave.

The streets seemed full of jagged split ends,
you felt there was serious cutting to be done,
so you tied up some schoolgirls and shaved their heads,
went home and watched the carpet growing long.

You were in the kitchen when the police came,
surrounded by heads - heads of lettuce, cabbage, cauliflower,
their leaves carefully trimmed, tidied up, neat. "A shame
to disturb him," the sergeant said as they led you to the car.

A year on and people don't notice you any more,
you're starting to come to terms with what happened,
when women walk past tossing their heads you look at the floor,
and now the sight of scissors doesn't make you too frightened.

With your hands in your pockets you look the same
as anyone else and no-one could guess you'd gone insane,
but certain things denounce you, like those scars which linger,
– the red indented rings round the thumb and forefinger.

The Lovers

We danced along the front,
we took up the tune of the sea,
tide pushed up beneath the pier,
seaweed hung like drowned men on the beams.

I felt something swell in me.
The moon washed itself in the dark water.

We lay down on the stones
to see the stars but none saw us.
Only the thick sea rolling over and over
watched us move there.

Slowly the night grew cold and cruel;
we watched the lights going out.
Then there was hard water on our faces,
hiding, filling mouths and noses, rushing over.
We held the moon's face down in the dark water.

Waiting

We came to the estate years ago,
two small kids put us top of the list.
A two up, two down with kitchen and bathroom,
a mud track for a garden.
It was nice then,
all the fronts with hedges,
and they were planting
those trees which line Almond Avenue.

Afternoons I waited at the gates
in a crowd of women,
weighed down with babies
in prams and the day's shopping.
The same old talk, gossip
like a soap, until the bell.
You can always spot your own,
could tell mine by the back of his head.

Never a day going past
without some small disaster.
You know how they are at school.
But at least each morning
I'd send them out with a clean shirt.
Never gave it a thought,
but I knew they'd be judged.
You get to hear it by the way.

And every year more complaints:
smoking, stealing, playing truant,
out all day up to god knows what.
Used to hope he'd come home when it rained,
but he never did.
Don't need to be told,
you can read it on their faces,
and smell it on their clothes.

No work after school, one experience,
no practice for what follows:
left home with some girl he met.
No wedding these days, only Sunday visits.
And the husband's cough getting deeper every morning,
-told me it would be over by Christmas.
One day I'm in the bedroom
quietly packing clothes.

Still see the same women
down the shops. On their own
or with their daughter's kids.
I remember standing with them by the gates,
slim in 60s fashions.
Times you pray for a quiet life,
but you've got your hands full
when the waiting is over.

raymond robinson
Yorkshire Dales, England

Migratory Birds

The little girl woke me by shoving Buzz Lightyear's hand
into my mouth. She put her face up to mine, her breath was
warm and sweet.

"Are you taking me to school now'?" she said.

I told her she still had another week before she started.

She pressed her nose against my cheek and whispered,
"Will you be my Daddy?"

I told her to go wake her mother up.

Later that day we were crouching on the edge of the moor
with plastic bags in our hands. The young girl shouted, "Here
I've found millions!" But it was just a pile of sheep droppings.

Her mother stood up and looked across the valley at the
other pickers.

"They're like migratory birds," she said. "From the end of
August to early November... where do they all come from?
The bastards don't even live here and they come and pick all
of our lovely mushrooms."

The young girl started singing across the valley at them,
"Ghetto poopy stars, that is what you are," and laughed at
herself.

That evening, suffused with the soft magic of the tea, I held
the sleeping girl in my arms and almost wished I was her
Daddy, but soon I would be leaving and knew that other
daddies would follow.

And Your Tongue fills Your Mouth

You're feeling dead good in your new short blue dress with the sun on your arms and face, walking through the busy market-day streets thinking about the skinhead guy who always plays the RidgeRider game waiting for you at the Mucky Duck. He asked you out yesterday, came up to your little booth, handed you a fiver and said,

Twenties and tens please and you want to go out sometime your name, what's your name err... hmm?

You started laughing and he scratched his head and you said,

Yes, Lisa, yes,

then he stood staring and said,

When?

and you said,

Tomorrow, Mucky Duck twoish,

then he stared again,

What is it? you said, and he frowned saying,

My change, please,

and you got all totally shy like and felt so daft. You pressed the levers and thechange slid down into the little metal tray at his side of the glass. He scooped it outand said, I've got the Top Three now, and strutted off proud as a dog with two cocks.

You didn't see him leave but when the arcade shut you went over to the machine. It read,

1 - 676,070,025 - - -
2 - 670,555,000 - - -
3 - 623,475,925 - - -

but there was no name, no initials. How cool was that.

Looking at the clock on the Town Hall you're late, so you're marching fast now, wishing some of the people inspecting the fresh-air and gobbing like goldfish would just *move,*

hey you, hippopotamus arse, MOVE IT

can't they see you're late, got a date with RidgeRider? Do you need to be covered in white fur and have big ears, to pull a watch from your waist-coat pocket and exclaim loudly oh dear oh dear, oh my EYES and WHISKERS, I shall be TOO late!

And though you've been back-heeling it to the rear of your thoughts it begins. Of all the times, of all the places. You stare down the street through the blur of heads towards the sea, smell the chip vinegar from Scarborough Fisheries, see the swathe of sputum green, the North Sea with the mucky grey seagulls dive-bombing above. Heeling it back. Wishing. No way. It's starting. The fitting. And in your new bloody dress. NO WAY.

Sometimes it's the lights
the world speeds up and you need to grab on to something like you've forgotten what gravity is and the Earth falls away from beneath your feet and you panic panic panic like fuck

God shouts BOO into your soul, his breath knocks you to the floor

you'll find somewhere to sit and take hold of someone's arm, bury your face into their breast, pull at their hair, snatch the child's doll away and chew its face off, rip the artist's sketch from the board and rip it to shreds all the time screaming

mmmmmgreeeeeheeeeeeyaaaaaNEEEEE

then panting like you're squeezing a baby elephant out your fanny and they, the strawmen and women, don't know whether to run cry hide or shite themselves, wondering if you're having a heart attack or a baby or just the latest Care in the Community fruitloop with your nails digging into the wooden bench or knuckles scraping the concrete steps till they bleed.

Sometimes there's no feeling at all
just the whambam, inhale, and dark electricity.

You spot a bench over by the fountain. A flatcapped old guy is sitting there with a mangy-looking sheepmutt, retired farmer type, and he smiles as you sit down and start to control the breathing, getting the kind of sick feeling, like you're gonna puke and it doesn't matter what position you stand or sit the rancid green waves come flooding over you. You don't know whether to stick your fingers down your throat or what.

You put your hands under your bum and bite your lips.

Feel it sizzling away in your head, remote static on a record, egg being fried in a distant kitchen.

Jesus it's coming. A strong one.

Soon you'll be down, supine on the concrete. No one really knows you in this town yet, which saves that extra bit of embarrassment. RidgeRider'll be nursing his pint and watching the door. You check the ground for dog crap, don't want to ruin the new dress more than you have to.

MMMMMgreeeee... ergh ergh ERRRRmmmm

You wrap your hands over your mouth.

They say you have the strength of ten men when fitting. Ten men. How many women is that? And they still don't know that much about it. You'll be on these pills till you peg it. Can't drive. Lots of things you can't do. You can make people laugh though. You don't blame them because it must look a bit funny: you on the floor shaking, choking on your tongue and pissing yourself, a grown-up doing that. Kids at school loved it.

Throwing an epi. Epi epi epi epi.

They scanned your head because you have this big lump on the left side above the ear. Da told you it's where Mum threw you down the stairs as a nipper when you wouldn't stop bawling one time and that's when the fits started. And the doctors came up with this none-too-bright idea that they should somehow try and 'pull you out' of the fit, because of the way your arms lock under the chin, and the bright sparks the doctors thought that by pulling your arms apart you'd be temporarily cured. And you can remember, about thirteen you were at the time and when you started fitting all of a sudden there'd be Mum and Da and whoever else was at hand trying to pull you out. But you were the Incredible Hulk, and they never did, and they gave up after that day you chucked about fifty fits, one after the other, and they had to get an ambulance.

FIT-TASTIC SPASTIC, that's what the kids at school called you.

mmmmmgreeeeeheeeeeyaaaaaNEEEEE

Now of course the old man's looking, as are two or three passersby. He probably wants to say something if he could only find

232

the words, but you just stare ahead making it more difficult for him.

HERRRmmmmm

Why don't these people just disappear? If you close your eyes hard enough and long enough could you wish them away like you did when you were a nipper?

Eyes closed, head spinning backwards, whoooo rodeo, you grab the old guy's jacket and pull him into you, still looking straight ahead.

You stare at the fountain, the crazy patterns the water's making, the sunshine making it sparkle like clear glitter nailpolish, reminds you of the car lights dancing across your bedroom ceiling at night. They're like little explosions which in their absence leave stars behind. This isn't an illusion, you're not seeing things for you've got tiny little glow-in-the-dark stars on the ceiling sent to you a couple of Christmases ago by a penpal in Australia. You marked out roughly the constellations known off by heart. The seven wee stars of the Big Bear, that's your favourite. You even tried to colour one of them in with a red felt pen, it being a red dwarf and all, but then it didn't glow and you had to replace it.

You remember the penpal telling you that he'd never seen the Big Bear, that things were different down there, they had a constellation called the Southern Cross which you'd never seen and that the shadow went across the moon the other way. Everything upsidedown and backtofront. It totally freaked you out. You used to write to him standing on your head.

You look at the stars at night till you fall asleep
they swim your dreams like a water snake.

Forever staring at the ceiling, at lights hanging from the ceiling, in the supermarket, the kitchen, the livingroom, the classroom, the Change booth at work, being wheeled on a trolley through the hospital corridors. Lights flashing, whirring past like on the machines in the arcade, the lights you cannot look at. The weight, the pressure, the buzz. Electricity passing through your body and you can hear eggs frying, brain cells fizzing. As if you're trying to shit through your skin, your pores. Shit it all out.

heeeeeyaaaaa ERRRGH ERRRGH

For a sillysecond you think it's going it's a false alarm and turn to see the old man's face mumbling something and you just smile and nod, your brain lopsided, head a sinking ship. You start squeezing his arm again and close your eyes. You know you're doing the squealing thing and it's gonna start speeding up soon. Is that sirens? Surely no-one's dialled yet? They're the worst, dick-heads with mobiles, fingers twitching on those buttons and you always feel like slapping them afterwards. JUST HANG ON A FUCKING TICK you want to shout but of course you can't. Then the paramedics give you such grief when you walk away, telling them to leave you the fuck alone, the crowd around interfering and all you want is to be invisible, to get home, changing into clean knickers and skirt.

A woman's voice, old, nosey old bag wants to know if yer alreet, luv.

If you can just get your breathing sorted it might go... just might pass.

hernyerrrGGGHHH hergh HERRR hergh

You once threw one and fell into the fire. You were about to get your tea, walking across the livingroom over the rug next to the fireplace, next to Da's chair where he'd always be perched in front of the telly with the remote in one hand and a B&H or a can of Special Brew in the other. Da. Useless fucking Da. Your proverbial armchair athlete, film-critic, politician, sports commentator, know-it-all voice of the masses. Fat bastard slob. He just stared. Sat there and stared, as if he hadn't seen it before, benumbed. You

234

of shirt, of skin. He seemed to take weeks to get out of his
chair - Ian Rush was probably in the goal area about to knock one
in. Givusa fuckin minute! he'd snarl. Then he grabbed your arms
and pulled you onto the hearthrug, struggling to turn you over, not
knowing whether to pat the burning out or run into the kitchen for
water.

You've still got the scars. Tommy used to run his tongue down
them, tickling. He said they were like four smooth worms
wriggling down your back and into your bum cheeks.

mmmm'greeeeeheeeeeyaaaaaNEEEEE

Oh it's coming now dead strong. You squeeze somewhere deep
inside you. The old man and some others have their hands on you
and the moonface woman's blowing bubbles fretting OH LUV
WHAT IS IT LUV and soon it'll come and you'll be lying in a
puddle of scent-marking piss and sweat, the people stood over you,
their faces looming out of the dark not knowing what the fuck to
do as you're on the floor, the old man trying not to look at your
knickers and pulling the dog off from licking you, and you recall
Mum spying on you from behind a stack of baked beans, hiding
from her little fucking embarassment she said.

Pick yourself up, you hear me? Pick yourself up! she shout-
whispered.

And if you don't piss yourself, which is highly unlikely, then
maybe RidgeRider won't mind you being late, maybe he's late too,
maybe you could rush home and change anyway, or just stick your
knickers in your bag, dry the back of the skirt under the
blowdryer in the ladies, spray some perfume on, right as rain. Eee
think of it: first date with no knickers. Maybe RidgeRider's the
one, maybe he won't mind, maybe

whambam, inhale, and dark electricity.

mark mcKain

California, USA

Next Time

"The next time we meet
let's keep our clothes on," I said
as I sucked her tongue
and bit her lip.
But it's hard to keep a promise
or think clearly
with your pants around your knees,
and the taste of her tongue, lip,
nipple are in the hollow
of your stomach, her breasts
are inside your eyes pushing out,
her hair is between your teeth.
Her collar bones click like bracelets
around your wrists,
her make-up coats your face
like caramel on an apple.

And the next time you meet
you will keep your clothes
on 5 or 10 minutes longer
before you pull and tear
at buttons, hooks,
hooks and leather belts.
Until you again have your prick
in her mouth, drinking, drinking,
sucking like infants at the sour
formula of what you have promised.
Until you forget what you said.
Until you forget
that you will never do this
with her again.

Satin

She was getting dressed.
I was five or six
hanging around my parents' bedroom.
I reached up to touch her
breasts. Father said I couldn't do that,
but Mother bent over so I could feel
her dark nipples -- soft, rich texture
like the satin edge of the blankets
on my bed I ran between my fingers.
I pushed one nipple. It retracted
inward like something mechanical.
When I squeezed, it popped out.
Repeat, repeat. I was greedy.

Mother pulled away. She hurried
to finish getting dressed to go out.
I ran to my room,
jumped on my bed,
pulled back the spread,
again ran the satin edge between my fingers,
savored the feeling.

Later, when I prowled topless beaches,
bars, popped the hook on another black,
push-up bra, I was opening a birthday present.
Satin, satin. Breathless.

geoff hattersley
Huddersfield, England

Handshake Poem

The summer's here, and the Managing Director
has just cleared out his desk, looking shaken
to be sacked for incompetence, and with rumours
of financial shenanigans and back-handers
laughed about openly on the shop-floor.

Last Christmas, he handed me a large box
of Cadbury's Milk Tray and said, glancing
at the name patch on my pale blue workshirt,
"Merry Christmas, Geoff", and shook hands with me
as though we were sealing a weapons deal.

And then, after catching me outside with a fag
when I should have been trimming lawnmower handles,
my first fag for three, nearly four long hours,
he gave me, some time in April or May,
my third written warning for misconduct.

The summer's here, and the Managing Director
has left the premises, his tail between his legs.
"They say he took a hundred grand from Battenfeld..."
We're all sure he's guilty, even if proved innocent.
Nothing could mar our ebullient mood.

Alex

I don't feel great
about the job I do
but I've got to
feel better than Alex.
On the Fourteen Hundred
making DC9 fans –
they're huge, heavy, very hot moulds
you can barely handle –
he suddenly shouts
"I HATE THIS BASTARD JOB!"
then places his hand
palm down on the table
and whacks it hard and loud
with a five-pound hammer.
It's the second time
he's broken a hand.
Previously, he punched
a concrete post.

Before and After Midnight

Wasn't *The Doors* a bloody stupid film?
I just laughed my head off at it.
I don't think I've ever liked a film less.

The telly's off, I smoke a cigarette.
Elsewhere, people rip pieces out of each other
in small, broke rooms of stink.

Beer and pig's breath. I decide to phone Nev
in Sweden, years of long-distance friendship hanging
between us like frayed ropes.

We're not in control of our destinies –
how the fuck did l end up here?
he says, I think, something like that.

Y'Know Warramean?

Everything he tells you
he follows with the phrase
Y'know warramean?
He's used to drinking every night
Y'know warramean?
I don't mean he goes out every night
he might just have a few cans in the house
Y'know warramean?
If he could get out of the habit of drinking every night
then he wouldn't have to drink every night
Y'know warramean?
And you feel like grabbing hold of him and shouting
I'M NOT THREE YEARS OLD, OF COURSE I KNOW WHAT YOU MEAN
Y'KNOW WARRAMEAN?
But you don't do that and he carries on
Y'know warramean?

He can't do overtime at the weekends
because of his Community Service
Y'know warramean?
He got done for almost nothing
well they called it assault
Y'know warramean?
I mean you can't call it assault
all he did was shout at her in the street
Y'know warramean?
Well she told the coppers he hit her
Y'know warramean?
Well he might have pushed her slightly
Y'know warramean'?
It's o.k., the Community Service
it'd be o.k. if you were getting paid
Y'know warramean?

Ride

To be honest, I didn't care for him,
but was willing to accept his offer
of a lift home after work in his car.

Trying to talk to him
was like selling snails
from door to door

so I stopped trying,
listened instead
to the latest dance music

on his loud radio.
I could just about stand it
after the noise of the machines all day,

the minutes and hours gone for good
with the whiff of sweat
and the voices of bosses.

Steve was twenty years old and the word was
he'd never done it with a girl.
I smiled and said thanks for the ride.

Randy Newman Et Al

The five greatest
living American
Jewish songwriters
have been in my ears
most of the weekend.
The sixth greatest
would have been too
only I'm not sure
who it is. Maybe
Neil Diamond...

I can hardly believe
I'm forty-two.
I feel fifteen or twenty-six
or thirty-eight
but never forty-two
or forty-one.

Like Harpo Marx

I spend my time standing in places like this
to make me the money that buys the things that are my things
once I've bought 'em, not some other fucker's.

They can beat you only if you take it
home with you - the job and all the bullshit.
Better to think about music, magic, something.

But you can't help thinking about *the place.*
I just die there, trying hard not to scream,
nodding my head like Harpo Marx.

I found out who it was did me place over.
They're in jail for car theft. Soon as they're out
I'm going to smack six shades of shit out of 'em.

The Valdez Blues

I had a plan, of sorts, listen to this —
I'd nail my penis to a wooden plank
like the saddest bastard who ever lived.

I was crazy no doubt, but how crazy
do you have to act before it matters?
There were crazier people in the world.

Thank God I had my plan, which seemed enough.
I was trying hard to concentrate
but my mind kept drifting off

to imaginary punk blues anthologies
and metaphysical Western movies,
sometimes starring Burt Lancaster.

At This Table In Huddersfield

I stare at the letter. It's from a young poet
who wants advice on how to get gigs in New York,
as if I could help him, at this table

barefoot in boxer shorts and a t-shirt,
the world's greatest harmonica player
filling my ears with not so simple blues

and Jeanette telling me
about a half-submerged supermarket trolley in the canal
and on the bottom, plastic traffic cones.

Yet more drivel about soap stars in today's rag.
They both enjoy sinks. They both eat radish.
"You paid money for this paper then, love?"

CARNEGIE HALL WITH TIN WALLS Fred Voss (Bloodaxe) pp 159 £8.95

reviewed by Fiona Arnott.

In this powerful collection Fred Voss writes about his life and work as a machinist in American aircraft manufacturing .The Goodstone Aircraft Company is the Carnegie Hall of the title, where skilled workers perform intricate acts of creation with brute force. It is a stage populated by diverse characters bullied into conformity by their colleagues and the system. It is a brutal environment which takes its toll on the employees both physically and mentally. Voss graphically chronicles what he experiences both in employment and, movingly, when he finds himself laid off. It is one of the paradoxes of these poems that however unattractive his employment, Voss finds it infinitely preferable to being out of work . It is almost a relief to the reader when Voss is rehired and his poems return to the daily grind.

The poems are espresso - short, strong and intense. Their unrelenting passion and tough talk can be overwhelming. There are few moments of beauty or tenderness, but when they do appear the contrast makes them more vivid and more poignant. 'Standout', a poem highlighting "The beautiful girl at the pipe bending machine" is an example of this. Her appearance is like discovering a diamond in a pan of grit. Women are mostly peripheral in this collection, either a shadowy lusted after secretary , an absent wife or pin-up reduced to body parts, yet here is a woman operating machinery alongside all the "sweating, strutting men". "How does she survive in this hostile environment?

Survival is an important theme. Clearly, some of his colleagues do not survive. Those who do are defiant. They are tougher than the rest . Black machinists sport Malcolm X t-shirts
> "as if to dare anyone to say anything about his wearing that shirt."
In 'The Stud', a gay colleague trains himself to "bench press 450 pounds" and waves a 50 pound lead hammer above his head.
> "For the first time in the machine shop's 20 year history, no one was telling any faggot jokes."
It would seem reasonable to assume that these workers would not

relish having a poet in residence.

Voss does not dwell on this, but some of the poems allude to how he is regarded - "They fear me." In 'The Criminologist', he is told that his

"…. quiet undercover never-speaking super-nice-guy
manner qualifies me as a possible PSYCHO…"

In 'A Threat', he decides to consolidate his image by bringing roses to work because

"I want to really terrify my fellow workers
this time"

The poems are parochial and they do contain occupational jargon, but they are effective because they say something relevant to everyone who has to work for a living in this day and age. Anyone who has felt their ideas have been disregarded by their employer, anyone who has health and safety concerns at work, anyone who has seen their place of work close down and their job relocated, will connect with Fred Voss. I found his disgust at corporate hypocrisy ('Ethical Giants'), his cynicism at sound - bite management techniques ('One Way Street') and irritation at meaningless abbreviations which are even less lucid when written in full ('Attacking The Problem') to be particularly pertinent.

These poems are strong stuff. Voss is a driven man with a passionate desire to write about his experiences. He does not attempt to dress it up. His poetry is not for the faint hearted. I wonder what his employers have made of his revelations about their business? I assume they are too busy to read poetry. I would also recommend that if you are a U.S fighter pilot and you happen to be reading this review,that you avoid *Carnegie Hall With Tin Walls.* You do not need to know all the details, but Voss reliably informs us that the manufacturers pay particular attention to the construction of your escape hatches.

Fiona Arnott

NEW BLOOD (Bloodaxe) pp 240 £9.95

reviewed by Fiona Arnott.

New Blood is an anthology edited by Bloodaxe founder Neil Astley.
Thirty eight poets are showcased, all of whom have had their first
collection published in the last decade.It is a remarkably diverse
and eclectic collection.Astley's introduction gives the statistics
about the cultural, academic and occupational breadth represented,
but dipping into the writers' pen pictures reveals amongst others a
former women's snooker champion, a machine operator, a journal-
ist and an ex-zoo keeper.One third of the writers are from the
North of England, a similar proportion are from Scotland and ten
were born or grew up outside Britain. Three quarters of those represented are women.

The poets are introduced with a photograph and a pen picture
including information about their publications. The writers have
also been given the opportunity to say something about their
inspiration and how they work. I liked this. It put the poems into
context without being mechanical or analytical and some of the
prose was as arresting as the poetry. (Pauline Stainer's idyll of
Orkney punctuated by the image of arctic skuas picking the eyes
out of live lambs had me going backwards just to check I'd got it
right - the lamb was alive?!). The idea is that the reader samples
and then wants to go further by purchasing particular collections.
Astley unashamedly describes anthologies as "Bloodaxe's shop
windows". If this sounds blatantly commercial, Bloodaxe is
determined to provide its readers with what they want not what
someone else thinks is good for them.Anthologies such as this allow
Bloodaxe to do that.

It does not seem fair for this review to highlight particular poets as
this would automatically preclude others. However, the poetry of
these thirty eight encompasses humour, political comment,
spirituality, rage, dramatic monologue, parody, personal experience
and everything in between. Among the subjects are football
hooligans, a secretary, a Northumbrian fisherman and there is
Lady Macbeth in an interesting twist on Shakespeare.There is a
liberal sprinkling of touchstones which show that these poets are

living in the here and now. We have the Gulf War, Chernobyl, pop lyrics and Ricki Lake. Whatever the subject, these poems make you feel - but they don't make you feel comfortable.

I have quoted from Astley's introduction because its honesty, commitment and sense of purpose are the glue which binds this diverse collection. I found his determination to make poetry accessible to a wider readership by drawing on poets from different backgrounds, striking and impressive. It is a determination which is amply reflected in *New Blood*.

SACRILEGE Brendan Cleary (Bloodaxe)

reviewed by Peter Knaggs.

The world needs more Brendan Clearys, more poets of
conviction. By conviction I mean that, he means what he says,
a too uncommon trait today. *Sacrilege* sees Brendan illustrat-
ing our everyday circumstances. Considering how much time
most of us spend in them, there aren't that many pub poems.
Cleary is on a one man crusade to redress this balance.
"The Lads," a totally refreshing piece of writing, no bandwagon
jumping, just honesty.
"Greg reckoned his marriage was up shit creek, completely,
with no paddle presumably, I added, he just
grinned."
Greg and the narrator soak up their hangover with a fry-up, no
political correctness for these lechers as they comment on the
passing females.

Sometimes quirky, odd or weird, "Planet Steve," is a personal
quest to befriend a Steve. In another mood he finds an
imaginative truth in suburban violence that Sophie Hannah
would give her last tub of humous for.
"Off Stage," "Katrina why are you holding that bread-knife to
his throat?" a scorcher of a first line.

Unswerving from a conversational style, his turn of words
is remarkably simple and moving, take, "Helen's Boyfriend,"
"If she marries this eejit I'll disintegrate."
or the comic timing unwinding in,
"Unhappy Hour,"
"So I asked her why she left,
It was because I am so ugly."

Song-lines intermittently sampled, *Sacrilege* sound-bites like a
film score, Brendan Cleary The Movie, The Soundtrack. It is
more than a good follow up to the slightly better, *Irish Card*. A
man of such pleasing complexity, what can I say? Julie Birchill,
here comes your man.

ON THE BUSES WITH DOSTOYEVSKY,
Geoff Hattersley (Bloodaxe)
reviewed by Peter Knaggs.

Geoff Hattersley is the popular editor of *The Wide Skirt*, one of
the most influential poetry magazines going. His new collection
is brim with observations nailing the tittle tattle, nitty gritty of
life today in Huddersfield. Or two thirds Huddersfield, the book
being divided into three, a kibbutz experience representing the
coronation chicken, sandwiched by the two slices of Huddersfield
bread.

The influences vary, the jacket notes point out Bukowski, but
this does Geoff an injustice. The line breaks and setting out on
the page nod more towards Frank O'Hara and as much could be
gleaned by studying Geoff's line endings as the poet's poet Paul
Muldoon.

Sometimes the everydayness turns into a weakness. At their
worst some of the poems leave you thinking, so what? But this is
the exception rather than the rule. Hattersley often, as in,
'About Something', binds the poems with camouflaged rhymes,
    "The life and soul of the party? Not you
  cold as pie in a dying man's fridge,"
brilliant, life and pie the pastry holding this poem together.

The final poem, 'Sunday Western', has tremendous energy,
triggered by the use of self as protagonist,
    "There are screwed-up beer cans on our path.
    They're mine, I threw them there. No one else did."

Full of character studies and narratives, a totally isolated voice,
I found my mind drifting to David Gedge more often than say
Armitage or Sweeney. I can't help feeling that today there are
not enough poets of vitality, not enough Geoff Hattersleys and
Brendan Clearys. We need more of this.

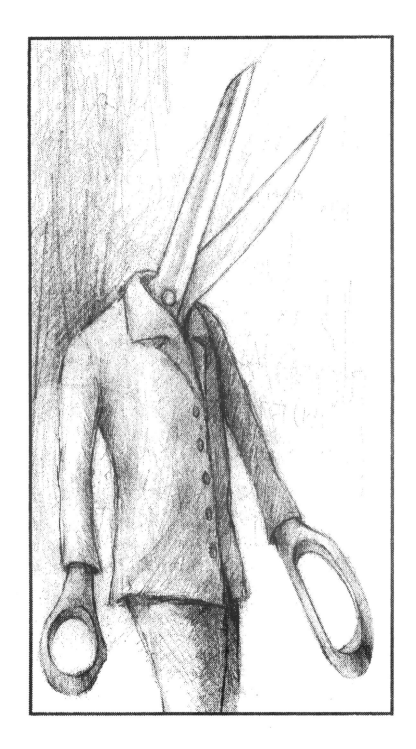